D1473712

FOREWARD

In this book, Jack Hayford offers something my heart desires for you and for every Christian: a clear and simple explanation of what it means to be "filled with the Spirit." By doing so, he removes, for anyone willing to listen, the confusion and anxiety surrounding the subject because of the way various Christian factions have misrepresented it.

Every sincere Christian should desire the experience of vibrant, Spirit-filled living. But they need to know what they are actually seeking and be willing to "stretch their sails" to receive it.

Jack Hayford will help you realize what many zealous Christians do not: that to be Spirit-filled is to be filled with all the fullness of God—the God who loves and works through all who love Him. As I often emphasize, a major element of being Spirit-filled is obedience to the "new commandment" Jesus

James Robison

gave us to "love one another." We cannot be filled inwardly unless we are emptying ourselves outwardly, loving others as He loves us—yes, even those whose beliefs differ from ours.

Dr. Hayford will help you understand another point I often stress and that is that such love does not—nor should it—result in either a doctrinal sameness or a monolithic organizational structure. Rather, it produces an atmosphere of spiritual unity that releases the power of God in each heart and in the Body of Christ. Remember, Jesus said, "You shall receive power when the Holy Spirit has come upon you" (Acts 1:8). To be filled with the person, power, love and dynamic life potential of Jesus is not only a possibility but a promise, not only a blessing but a necessary experience.

With his winsome ability, Jack Hayford will stir your heart to catch the wind of the Spirit and allow your life to be expanded until it holds all the fullness of God. You will find his invitation all the more appealing coming, as it is, from one who has first stretched his own sails.

A
PASSION
for FULLNESS

JACK
HAYFORD

Spiritual *Life* Library

A Passion for Fullness

Printed by LIFE Publishing
LIFE Outreach International
P.O. Box 982000
Fort Worth, Texas 76182-8000
817/267-4211

Printed in the United States of America

To the Missionary Pioneers I have known,

whose passion for Christ took them to distant nations over a generation ago to evangelize in hostile environments in the raw power of the New Testament's most basic spiritual resources; and

who penetrated *hidden people groups* before that term was coined and transformed *third world nations* when missiology was not a science and when transportation, communication and economic support made their fields of ministry as difficult to reach as they were an unwelcome place to live by human terms.

They constitute a holy legion "of whom the world was not worthy" and the whole of all such known only in heaven. However, the force of witness by a few of them not only has shaped the history of the nations which they touched, but impacted my life and ministry. To these I especially dedicate this book:

to Evelyn and Arthur Thompson, who ignited the Island of Mindanao as torches fired by the Holy Spirit of God;

to Jean and John Firth, who exploded demonic strongholds in Colombia to clear the way for widescale evangelism;

to Barbara and Leland Edwards, who have lived out the essence of that servant-spirit which lays life down that multitudes may live; and to

the Joe Knapps, the Claude Updikes, the Mason Hughes, the Herman Mitzners, the Bill Pritchetts, the Edwin Gurneys, the Thomas Andersons, the Frank Zieglers, the George Faulkners, the Harold Curtises, and the saints like Mattie Sensabaugh,

who each—along with unnamed others—moved in the power of the Holy Spirit fullness and Christlike self-sacrifice that people hopelessly lost would be eternally saved.

These all accomplished mighty spiritual exploits, and while doing so they also overflowed something of the life and power of the Holy Spirit which helped begat in me a continuing passion for "all the fullness of God."

CONTENTS

INTRODUCTION

Before We're Done ... Before We Start

Before we're done I must tell you about the day I buried my face in a pillow. But before we start I want to tell you about a more recent day I buried my head in my arms.

The "face in the pillow" episode occurred with my coming to "face up" to a point of personal discovery. The "head in my arms" took place for quite another reason.

Frustration. Helplessness. Pressure.

All three welled up and around me as I was laboring to bring this book to completion. I was wanting to write a far more "cerebral" book than this has turned out to be. I wasn't craving a self-verifying intellectual image of some type, but I did feel a desire to give a reasoned definition of "fullness."

I was *very* hopeful of presenting a broad-spectrumed view of Bible-based, Holy Spirit "fullness," which would seem neither sectarian or separatist. So often the subject seems to polarize and fragment; to *splinter* rather than to *splice*.

So, I intended to show how the primary themes of Christian life and truth integrate with a singularly passionate spiritual quest for Spirit-filled living. I hoped to link spiritual "passion" to scriptural precepts; to show *both* the *foundations* in truth and the *fullness* realized when passion pursues the potential for power inherent in sound doctrine. Through discussing *doctrines* of Christian faith as the basics for *dynamics* of Christian living, I was aiming to show that an impassioned pursuit of God and His wonder workings in our generation is not a mindless meandering of mystically misguided saints. But I soon discovered something I should have known before I started.

Passion is far more visceral than cerebral!

I *have* done what I planned in touching doctrinal themes, but I still concluded with a book which I think may prove more *moving* than mental.

Movement.

Forward.

The words bespeak a lifestyle for the vibrant Christian, because Jesus—Who *is* "The Way"—is *always* calling us to follow Him. Reading the journals of faith's champions, we find that to effectively and fruitfully follow Christ is to answer a lifelong summons to new horizons. There's a certain unsettledness with any serious disciple. It is not the unsettledness of erratic faith or behavior, but an unpredictability—a readiness to "go where You want me to go, dear Lord . . . be what You want me to be."

Since Abraham, the first to "go out, not knowing where," the faith-life has always been described as a journey—a pilgrimage. To settle for something less than *movement*—cutting-edge Christianity—and then to call it "stability" may give it the *sound* of orthodoxy. But true orthodoxy is found in that flexibility of soul which refuses only to know the truth—it insists on *experiencing* it as well.

Insistence on experience is not shallow sensation-seeking, nor is the flexibility of soul to which I refer a spinelessness which bends to suit the latest spiritual fad. Instead, it integrates all experience with a sound body of systematically revealed truth which provides trustworthy underpinnings for the follower's faith-walk. Thus, wise spiritual pioneers, who are willing to venture forward in vital discipleship, are never casual about the doctrinal verities which provide timeless grounds for their currency in spiritual experience.

I wanted to *affirm* the solid ground of Scripture undergirding great themes, while *asserting* our call to experience the powerfilled, promise-packed implications of those truths. And I think I have succeeded in expressing my passion that we both *know* and *glow* the truth. But as I proceeded to write, I was drawn more and more to the *passionate* side of this issue—to the *glowing* more than the *knowing*. That bothered me—partly because of a phantom person I thought it would bother. That human specter in my mind was an enemy to my thesis; a cynic whose jaundiced eye would only see froth in my faith and superstition in my quest for the supernatural.

Then something changed.

I buried my head in my arms in prayer and, after this simple request for His help, the Lord removed that phantom. I grew less dubious, less threatened, less fearful of criticism, for I realized these pages were addressing *you*—a person whose heart, I expect, is much like mine:

- We love Jesus Christ, sincerely and in truth;
- We prize God's Word, being committed to its authority;
- We want God's Spirit to fill life and living.

So I have written you. (That *is* you I just described, isn't it? I presume so, because I can't imagine anyone picking up a book by this title who doesn't already feel something of the pulse of that pursuit.)

Though I began planning to spend far more time defining the fullness of *doctrine*, I have become more concerned about this central passion—a fullness of *dynamic*. But while urging that passion, I steadfastly insist that such a pursuit is not a quixotic quest ending in dreamy mysticism or lopsided living.

- *This passion is for everyone* to know that vibrant Spirit-filled living is not a slightly aberrant, arbitrarily pursued lifestyle, sought only by fanatics and zealots.
- *This passion is for everyone* to know that Bible-centered living is not an antiseptic system prescribed by precept but without daily dynamism.
- *This passion is for Christians of every tradition* to agree that biblical balance and spiritual vibrancy are neither mutually exclusive nor is one to be preferred above the other.

Thus, the "passion" part got the best of me and I have ended up writing more about it than about precepts.

Perhaps I am doomed to the critics' ban for not being weighty enough. Perhaps I've been too superficial—failing to probe the depths of doctrinal issues which deserve study and elaboration beyond the space this book allows. But as I evaluated that possibility another "perhaps" occurred to me.

Perhaps God is far more interested in our personal passion *for* Him than He is in our academic perceptions *about* Him.

Frankly, I think that's true. Not because I'm indifferent toward the values of study, scholarship, systematic theology, or solidly grounded understanding. Rather, it's because I believe God is far more interested in finding *passionate* people who desire His life and love than He is in cultivating *precise* people who stop after describing His being and their beliefs.

If you even *suspect* as much, you're already a part of a vanguard.

There are multitudes who are making vital discoveries about Christ's love and power for today. The church on the edge of the Third Millennium is exploding with new life on the frontiers of nations where twenty centuries of witness have made little impact. At the same time, renewal throbs in virtually every sector of the church in the Western world, where historically ensconced tradition is being infused with new life before it withers into colorlessness.

Earnest hearts, longing to move with wisdom as well as power, have watched the insurgency of the Spirit's gifts and miracle signs.

God is undeniably at work, manifesting Book-of-Acts operations of His grace everywhere. In doing so, He often contradicts and confounds many of His own servants.

- He *contradicts* any of us who have doubted the contemporaneity of the miraculous.
- He *confounds* all of us who accept His signs and wonders, but who thought we knew all the rules by which He operates.

People who care wrestle with these facts. They care enough not only to *want* God's workings of power in their midst, but enough to want God's Word honored at the same time.

So, I write to *thinking* Christians who want to center everything in the Word and on its truth—and to *thoughtful* Christians who know that spiritual truth is more than simply thoughts and that God's Word is more than mere words.

My heart quest is to balance the two sources which bring fullness—The Spirit and The Word. If I have not addressed either sufficiently—of the Word's *objective* revelation or the Spirit's *subjective* operations—I trust you'll forgive me.

I arrived here after putting my head into my arms—to pray. Come with me, if you will. In awhile I'll tell you about the pillow.

In His faith, hope and love,

Jack W. Hayford

The Church On The Way
Van Nuys, California

CHAPTER

1

But all things are naked and open to the eyes of Him to whom we must give account. Hebrews 4:13

Being "On the Stretch" for God

The sun had not yet risen above the horizon of the mid-Michigan plain, although the sky was light and birds had already begun their morning song. As I quietly slipped from the bed and dressed silently so as not to disturb my wife, I felt a deep hunger that no breakfast on earth could satisfy. It was an appetite created by a feast the night before.

It had only been four months since I had completed my studies for the ministry and immediately set forth on a series of youth evangelistic services scheduled throughout the Great Lakes region of the United States. As I stepped outside onto the porch of the parsonage where we were guests for the duration of the present meetings, I studied the landscape, feeling a rising thrill of expectation.

I wanted to go somewhere and pray.

The evening before, after we had enjoyed fellowship with the local pastor and his spouse, I had stopped in his study to look over his bookshelf. It was there I found a small volume which was destined to impact my soul as no other one of human authorship. It was a book which not only had caused my early rising on this day, but whose message would continue to ring in my spirit till the present. More than anything else in that profound, pithy and powerful piece, one phrase throbbed within: "We need to be on the stretch for God."

The Preacher and Prayer by E.M. Bounds[1] spoke to me, *not* of a "stretching" of human effort or creative enterprise in ministry, but of a stance of the soul which refuses *ever* to take comfort in the shape of things as they are—within or without. Whether the issue in question be the condition of one's own spirit—healthy or otherwise—or the circumstances in the world around—stressed or peaceful—I was persuaded: a man "on the stretch" was God's avenue of action.

Jesus' words about *wineskins* describe this same summons to "stretchability." Early I learned the tendencies of my own soul to settle for the status quo; to relax on the record of whatever gains experience or understanding had brought me. Nothing in my training had prepared me for battle with the greatest monster threatening abounding fruitfulness in my life. That beast isn't lust, greed, conceit or error; it's the unperceived smugness that drugs the soul with the notion that our boundaries of understanding God are the boundaries of His readiness to reveal Himself to us.

In His parable of the wineskins, the Master confronts our soul's comfort zone. He isn't asking us if we think we *know* everything. We know too much—and too little—to suggest we do. But instead, He's asking how much we are willing to receive of *Him*—of the *newness* of His Spirit *today*! After all, new wine isn't pressed just once in a lifetime. People of His Vine must regularly candidate themselves for a new outpouring, season after season.

ALL OVER THE EARTH
Who can number the "seasons of refreshing" in Christ's church since Pentecost when the new wine first gushed forth? The Creator Himself has proved as prolific in providing fresh

spiritual stimulus for the church as His natural realm of agriculture has provided recurrent grape harvests. During the twentieth century alone, no fewer than four distinct globe-encompassing seasons of renewal have touched the church. With and besides these, regional visitations of the Spirit of God have been registered like seismic events at thousands of locations where God's people have been ready and willing to be *stretched*—to drink in new wine, even if its presence burst the boundaries of their comfortable Christianity.

Each successive wave of worldwide outpouring forces an answer to the question: "Was the Reformation a climax or a commencement?" Was the reinstatement of justifying truth to culminate in an ensconcement of self-justifying unavailability to future renewals? There is no question that the God of the Reformation is "a mighty fortress," but He also reveals Himself "like a mighty wind." Yet, too easily, behind my *own* fortress walls, I may insulate myself from the fresh breezes of heavenly breakthrough as they waft from season to season. Whether the metaphor is wind or wine, the fact is that both stretch us—the sails of our soul, the skins of our habits.

On a rising wave of renewal, the Church is cresting toward a "New Reformation." This one needs to be as liberating from heirarchal resistance to the believer's passion for Holy Spirit fullness, as the first Reformation liberated believers from ecclestiastical oppression 500 yrears ago. In that awakening, people were freed to know Jesus—to experience the forgotten joys of forgiveness and God-intended peace through justifying grace. In a 21st century awakening, may every Christian be freed to know the Holy Spirit—to experience the first-century joys of praise and God-intended power through overflowing grace.

We aren't surrendering to the frothy prognostications of journalistic rags or to the dreamy mysticism of the New Age's prophets when we allow such hope to rise. Those dreams of a divinely destined era of unprecedented global impact of the gospel of Jesus Christ are born of the Holy Spirit. The Living Christ is at work, stretching the souls of His saints to make room for the mighty things He is ready to do *through* them. The grace He pours toward mankind flows through the vessels of those who already are His own—His church. Thus, His broadest workings await the willingness of His own to be stretched to broader dimensions of His grace, His power, and His wonder workings. In short, the Bride of Christ can hardly expect to reproduce aboundingly unless she is willing to be *stretched*; and like a woman during pregnancy, the process isn't comfortable.

POSSESSED BY A PASSION

The analogy of childbearing is neither misguided nor unscriptural. Isaiah prophesied of Zion's travail unto birth; Jesus spoke of the church age involving convulsions like a woman in labor; and Paul urges us toward a walk in Holy Spirit fullness which begets contractions of intercessory prayer promising the birth of God's purposes through the church.

A Passion for Fullness is not merely a quest for an exhilarating swig of spiritual excitement; it's a pursuit of *all* the fullness of God! But who can plumb those depths or search those boundaries? "Oh, the depth of the riches both of the wisdom and knowledge of God! How unsearchable are His judgments and His ways past finding out!" (Romans 11:33).

And yet such disclosures of His grandeur have never been intended to stifle our search or promote a passive acquiescence to the flesh's ready will to set its own limits on God. We do this, not of the mind that our strength could ever withstand His, but in the blind insistence, "If He wants to do more in me, I'm perfectly open—but it's up to Him. After all, He *is* sovereign!"

But Jesus' own words contradict such passivity. Sovereignty, on Christ's terms, never meant to argue man's resignation to a divinely ordered scenario, pre-scripted to write out man's role in the drama. He said, "Blessed are those who hunger and thirst after righteousness, for they shall be filled." There are few passions that exceed the human desperation for food and water. Fullness follows the passionate quest: the Sovereign God waits to reveal His fullness to those who seek Him.

To this day, New Testament translators labor with Matthew 11:12 and Luke 16:16—

> And from the days of John the Baptist until now the kingdom of heaven suffers violence, and the violent take it by force (Matthew 11:12);
> The law and the prophets were until John. Since that time the kingdom of God has been preached, and everyone is pressing into it (Luke 16:16).

The problem exceeds ambiguity of grammatical construction; it's as much about theology as it is about syntax or verb tenses: We all have difficulty with the proposition that God has left so much of the issue in our hands—that "kingdom breakthrough" should be awaiting the passion of the violent seeker. Since we know that *His* is *all* "the kingdom and the power and the glory," how is it He so restricts Himself to the passion of His people? But that is precisely the status of the whole redemptive process: His is the commission and the power for its fulfillment; ours is the responsibility and the need for the fullness which will complete the mission.

However, at each band on the spectrum of Christian personal experience, historical tradition, doctrinal persuasion, liturgical exercise or denominational polity, virtually everyone considers *his* or *her* stance toward Christian life and service as representing a "full" or complete position. Any group *pre*-dating the Reformation era will hold that they have held to the "faith once delivered to the saints," while those groups conceived in various reforms, revivals or renewals *since* then perceive themselves as having *recovered* what the others either overlooked or forfeited. Who among us fellowships in a church that would even suggest for a moment that we need "something more"?

STRETCHED BEYOND THE SECTARIAN

Most of us are constrained by the influence of unwritten laws and unspoken demands which invisibly shape our lives and thoughts until we become more controlled by categories and conditions than we even begin to realize.

One of the most bewildering conversations I ever had took place with my parents shortly before my entry into the ministry. Harking back to those few minutes of my life, I hardly know how to adequately praise God for the seed that was sown by my mother's comment.

We stood in the kitchen as she proceeded with her preparation of the noontime meal:

"Well, son, now that your studies are completed, how are you feeling about your preparation for the Lord's work?"

"I feel good, Mama," I replied. "It's a very exciting thing to be ready to go out now, to teach and to preach with confidence that I have a message that will completely meet the need of human hearts and lives."

"That's fine," she said, "I'm glad. But I want you to remember one thing. Nobody has a 'corner' on truth."

I understood her use of the word "corner" in the classic stock-market usage; in other words, no group controls *all* the shares. My response to her betrayed a place in my soul which had already begun to shrink during my years of theological training.

She was bent before the oven, placing a tray inside, her back to me as I spoke: "You mean, of course, don't you Mama, 'Nobody who lacks the full gospel message *we* preach'? You surely don't think *we're* deficient of something of the *whole* Word of God."

I've never forgotten her next words or action.

She slowly stood erect, looking at me with grave intensity. Not unkindly but with a deep and penetrating gaze, her eyes spoke infinitely more than even her measured words could have: "Jack," she paused, a patient intensity in her voice, "I said *nobody*."

I was momentarily shaken by the conviction with which she addressed the matter. I knew she wasn't simply speaking to me; she was venting a concern that had obviously come from many years of serious reflection. I knew her commitment to Christ, to the Word, to loving, serving and giving; and I knew her reasoned response was born of experience which mandated more than mere parental respect.

We discussed the matter more fully that day, as I debated the question: "What more could there possibly be? Certainly *others* hold different positions than *we* do, and *they* would have ideas *we* certainly *don't*, but since they are certainly 'wrong,' then our *not* having *their* tenet of faith or practice in *our* system certainly doesn't mean *we lack* anything!" Mama wasn't argumentative, but she held her ground. I concluded that conversation unconvinced, but a crack had appeared in the dike.

As years have passed, I'm sure I have not been sufficiently sensitive or insightful to be rid of all my sectarianism. How many of us have been explicitly trained or attitudinally conditioned to believe that to concede to any doctrinal position at variance with ours (however Christian it might even be!) shows either a character weakness or a suspicious bent toward heresy? Is it possible my security in Christ is more founded in an intellectual conviction of my "being right" than in the spiritual reality that His Cross has made me righteous?

Years of "stretching" have increasingly limbered up the tightness of my system and widened my perspective on Christ's great, global body, and I have come to appreciate the wisdom of Trueblood's maxim: "He who begins with loving his own view of truth more than the truth itself, will end in loving his own denomination more than Christ, and ultimately in loving himself most of all."

I recently sat at lunch with a renowned expositor, and though we had just met, he was quick to indicate parameters to our fellowship. "Jack," he said pointedly, "you'll find I live a very clearly circumscribed life." His mood was not unkind. The smile on his face indicated that our friendship was allowable. I'm not even sure how much he meant to tinge our first meeting with the atmosphere of tentative or conditional acceptance.

But I've unwittingly done the same to others, doubtless in more conversations than I realize, and only discovered my unkindness too late. How can I forget the teary eyes of a Methodist pastor who gently asked me why I had made a passing comment in a lecture, slurring the relative "evangelistic zeal" of that great movement? How can I escape responsibility for the pain I caused a young preacher when a remark I made at a conference seemed to mock one of his Pentecostal group's traditions? His well-controlled anger was hardly allayed, and his insistent "Why?" elicited my immediate apology. But from that moment on, I was cautioned by my capacity for causing unintended injury to Christ's body.

FULLNESS BY WHAT MEASURE?

My confession contains an inquiry and a heartcry.

If indeed we are at a new and dynamic juncture of the church's two-millennia history, and if indeed our answering this hour requires more stretch in our souls to contain more fullness of God's Spirit and power, by what standard shall we measure that "fullness"? Paul's words to the Ephesians point to a state of sanctification in a believer's life. But might they also point to an era in the church Christ is building? ". . . until we all come to the unity of the faith and the knowledge of the Son of God, to a perfect man, to the measure of the stature of the fullness of Christ . . ." (Ephesians 4:13).

What is that unity of the faith to which we are called? Is it complete interdenominational agreement on doctrine? Worldwide acceptance of ecclesiastical structure? A syrupy love spread over a watery syncretism?

Of course not!

But neither can "the unity of the faith" be attained without a willingness to embrace its goal—"*the fullness of Christ.*" In the last analysis, the church will only be united around *Him*, never around its statements of faith. Once again, Jesus is stepping into the middle of His disciples' arguments. To those ready to call fire down on their apparent enemies, He is still saying, "You know not of what spirit you are . . . ." Others of us, like the beloved John, may need a fresh exposure to another of His discipling statements:

Now John answered Him, saying, "Teacher, we saw someone who does not follow us casting out demons in Your name, and we forbade him because he does not follow us." But Jesus said, "Do not forbid him, for no one who works a miracle in My name can soon afterward speak evil of Me. For he who is not against us is on our side" (Mark 9:38-40).

Jesus' heartcry will later be, "Father, that they may be one." But here, much earlier in His ministry, the Savior labors to break the sectarian spirit of either smallness or superiority: the snobbishness that poisons the world scene and deserves no presence in the church. But the fullness of Christ's Spirit in us all *can* crowd out the smallness that threatens us. His Spirit *will* disallow my "calling down fire" on those who reject me, and will teach me to accept as "on my side" those who love and serve the true and living Jesus, however different their style of "casting out demons" (i.e., their efforts at evangelism or serving Christ).

Where shall we find a beginning point of conversation on the question, "What constitutes 'fullness' of ministry?"

Historically, each wave of revival or renewal sweeping through the earth leaves a deposit of blessing and, for those most central to that season's visitation, a new "high-water mark." This is seen in the fact that every revival begets new groups, organizations, denominations or nondenominated entities—all of which take their birthmark from that respective visitation. By reason of that fact, the tendency of each "new wave" is to doubt the currency or effectiveness of any group born during an earlier sweep of divine grace. Then, the "compliment" is returned by the earlier-formed group—sides are taken, lines drawn and each one's definition of "fullness" becomes standardized by the "high-water mark" of each respective entity's experiential or doctrinal requirement.

The result is more than the sadness of mere division; it is the tragic loss of *gain*. Might it be possible that the church could *gain* perspective, breadth and depth with each tidal wave of divine blessing—accumulating the benefits of history's best workings of God while keeping open to His freshest outpourings?

At the turn of this century, an insightful writer paralleled the *demise* of the church's power-life—from the diminishing of the early brightness into the dark ages—to Israel's locust-ruined fields in Joel's day. Then she saw the returning *rise* in renewal and restoration—like the restoration beginning with the Reformation—as analogous to Joel's prophesied "spring rains" which would bring renewed life and full fruitage to the fields, climaxing in a bountiful harvest. The genius of the insight was that, over the seasons of refreshing, nothing was discarded in the growing flow of the Holy Spirit's reforming, reviving, renewing and restoring process.

Today the church is being called to accept the ancient standard: "Be filled with all the fullness of God" (Ephesians 3:19). Such a degree of His fullness can hardly be expected to distill in our souls if we insist He only blesses us to the dimension of our private circles. We are wise to share in the facets of fullness with which He is blessing the *whole* body of Christ; to cease our pretensions of self-sufficiency apart from *fully* receiving His grace in biblical ways that are being seen around the world. Only blindness of soul can allow us to stand apart—persisting in our "private world"—while others insist on their superior maturity or revelationary insight.

The definition of "fullness" is neither superiority nor maturity, but *stretchability*. It means we have allowed the Holy Spirit to renew the wineskins of our souls, to expand the vision of our understanding, to enlarge our heart for Christ and His redeemed, and to extend our reach to the world.

Joel prophesied that a "final harvest" will be reaped some day. Whether it will be in our time remains to be seen, but this much is sure: it will be harvested by those upon whom the Holy Spirit is outpoured at a measure of fullness unrealized by any previous generation since Pentecost. It will be a measure of fullness that is received by people too thirsty for God to mind the fact that the taste of new wine is never as mellow as the old.

Their passion for "all the fullness of God" will peel back the self-righteous garments of dependency on even the finest human systems, and standing naked before God they shall shine in the glistening rains of the fresh fullness Jesus promises to all who hunger and thirst.

Let us come together and share all we have each received.

Let us be stripped of all pride in what we have privately accumulated.

And let us stand like children rejoicing in the rain. Then, being girded by grace, let us go and garner the harvest God's latter rain brings.

CHAPTER

2

But I know that when I come to you, I shall come in the
fullness of the blessing of the gospel of Christ. Romans 15:29

A Passion for Fullness

The 4,000-seat, multilevel congress hall was packed, and nearly 1,000 men and women had overflowed into the adjacent auditorium where the press and other participants viewed the proceedings via closed-circuit television. More than 180 nations were represented by select evangelical church leaders as 5,000 men and women gathered in Manila for Lausanne II—the Congress on World Evangelism.

More than eight months earlier I had been pleasantly surprised to be designated as one of those privileged to represent my nation at this Congress, but also amazed to be asked that I speak at one of the evening plenary sessions. My assigned topic: "The Power of the Holy Spirit in World Evangelism." With it came the explicit directive: that I specifically deal with the ministry of the miraculous as well as the gifts of the Holy Spirit.

Reflecting on the history of the Lausanne movement, I realized that the planners of this Congress were manifesting a remarkable openness toward a broadening mutuality in the global body of Christ. When Billy Graham had called the first such Congress in 1974, the Covenant resulting from that gathering indicated a beginning point for blending. The historic cleavage between traditional and mainline evangelicals, as contrasted with Pentecostal and charismatic evangelicals, had been addressed with a cautious sensitivity. The gracious and embracing statement distilling from that earlier meeting indicated the possibility that "all" the Holy Spirit's gifts may indeed be as valid for the church's contemporary ministry as at any time in the first century.

Now, fifteen years later, with the accumulated evidence of massive evangelistic results accruing through Pentecostal and charismatic missions, and it being attested to by solid, unbiased researchers, there was an even greater willingness to hear of what the Holy Spirit is saying and doing in the whole church. The direct placement of such a topic at so conspicuous a location in the ten-day Manila Congress program was a statement of its own. The third night of the gathering, the Holy Spirit's *full* ministry would be addressed: both in *conversion* and in *charismata*—in *His power to transform* the human soul and beget Christlike character and in *His power to confirm* the Eternal Word with signs following unto evangelistic breakthrough.

I was humbled by the invitation to be a messenger for this occasion, and I felt a matching sense of privilege when I realized who my speaking partner would be. In the world of Christian scholarship, no name outshines that of Dr. James I. Packer, the renowned British theologian now serving on the faculty at Regent College in Vancouver, Canada. Though we had never met, I felt that I knew him well through his writings. His wisdom and insight into the Word of God have made him beloved among multitudes, but his notable graciousness of spirit was what most encouraged my heart as we approached that evening.

Dr. Packer was assigned to speak first, dealing with the Spirit's work in conviction and conversion. I was to follow with the Spirit's power and resources for the ministry of evangelism. I was at peace in the knowledge of several things which liberated my spirit as I rose to preach:

- First, I had been *asked* to address the theme at hand, and was trusted to be direct without being divisively "pushy" with the truth.

- Second, James Packer, while a non-charismatic, had always shown a gentle and biblical willingness to acknowledge real values in the Pentecostal/charismatic revival.

- Third, my manuscript had been reviewed a full three months earlier by the program committee. Dr. Packer himself, who had been given a review copy, had said, "I was grateful for your letter, and very happy with your draft address—mine is heavily cognitive; yours is heavily inspirational, and the two together ought to make, under God, a worthwhile evening's ministry. I am very happy with the way you express yourself, as I said above: I do not have the problems with manifestations that some do. You will minister with the authority of your significant church ministry behind you— and, I know, in the power of God. It will be a pleasure to prepare the way for what you have to say. I will pray for you."

- Fourth, I sensed something of the Savior's own pleasure with the moment. That was entirely separate from my own participation, for I was incidental to the chemistry of the circumstance. But *Jesus* was there, and He was ready to *do* something as well as to *speak* to us by the Holy Spirit.

As Dr. Packer concluded a marvelously sensitive and scholarly development of the Holy Spirit's work in bringing us unto Christ and into Christ, a brief interlude allowed for the transition to the companion message and my introduction as speaker. After giving appropriate acknowledgments, I briefly referred to the fact that the program committee had made a secondary request when asking me to bring this message: When the message was ended, I was to lead the Congress in a season of prayer and worship, both with singing and with direction in a prayerful response to the Word of God.

I was not prepared for the results of that arrangement of things.

As I preached, I sensed the warm, affirming touch of the Holy Spirit's presence; but when I concluded there was an unusually strong attendance of grace; indeed, many reporters described what happened as a strong confirmation—a visitation of God's power. But not all would agree. Questions would abound the following day—and while elements of conflict would seek entry, a gracious resolution would result from wise leaders insisting on our being broad in our acceptance of God's various ways of working among and through us all. According to many analysts, it was a watershed event. I don't know if that's true, and obviously I would be reticent to say so even if it proved to be. But it was a deeply moving experience to be asked to address this demanding theme to this discerning audience.

I titled my message, "A Passion for Fullness," taken from the texts:

> But I know that when I come to you, I shall come in the fullness of the blessing of the gospel of Christ (Romans 15:29).

> . . . that He would grant you, according to the riches of His glory, to be strengthened with might through His Spirit in the inner man, . . . to know the love of Christ which passes knowledge; that you may be filled with all the fullness of God (Ephesians 3:16, 19).

I BEGIN THE MESSAGE . . .

My assigned part in addressing the subject of "The Power of the Holy Spirit in World Evangelism"—*my assigned theme*—brings us to the realm of the miraculous—to signs, wonders and spiritual gifts. The objective of this message is not to overlook or minimize any other aspect of our ministry, but to help us hear the call of the Holy Spirit to receive His supernatural works and gifts unto a new release of power in our witness.

Jesus said of the Comforter's coming, "He will testify of Me and you also will be witness . . . " (John 15:26). Most simply defined, the word "witness" means "to bear testimony"; that is "to give evidence for the case"; so evangelism is *both* in the conveying of a message *and* the demonstration of the Spirit's power.

Thus described, the Word of God reveals that the gospel indeed comes as a two-edged sword: *first*, by declaring that Jesus died for our sins and rose again according to the Scriptures; and *second*, by confirming the Word with evidences of power, proving Jesus *is* still alive and active—saving the lost, transforming the soul, healing the sick, and delivering the demonized.

A passion for fullness in such ministry may well rise in us all. Without such fullness we draw on less than the resources we need to shatter hell's strongholds and answer human need.

I address this theme feeling much like the blind man Jesus healed. As with him, I claim no superior wisdom or accomplishment, but only that I've seen the result of Jesus' miracle working. I think we *all* know how that man felt. He's a biblical case of McCandlish Phillips' comment that "a man with an experience is never at the mercy of a man with an argument."[1] Just as we all have an *experience* of salvation and not only a theology, so I've tasted the Holy Spirit's actual miracle power in evangelism, healing and deliverance.

More than fifty years ago as an infant I was healed of a life-threatening affliction. Our family physician frankly told my parents that my healing was unexplainable apart from God. Shortly after this, my parents were converted at the church which had prayed for my healing.

Later, I contracted polio, and was healed through the anointing and prayer by our church elders. So it is by God's miracle grace that my family was born again, that I can walk, and that I stand before you now.

As a teenager, I answered God's call to the ministry. Because I was a result of them, I committed to a ministry allowing for and expecting Christ's miracles, signs and wonders. Even though I have often been disturbed by excesses and fanaticism among some who exercise such gifts, I have stayed in this community because I found that for every instance of excess there are a hundred examples of depth, reality and divine power.

Contrary to our preconceptions, God is *not* economical with healings and miracles. Such wondrous works are frequently attending the proclamation of the truth in Jesus' Name. I do not suggest that church growth *only* occurs where signs and wonders are experienced, but as the Holy Spirit's gifts proliferate, evangelism expands and results in church growth.

Growth in hundreds of congregations vastly exceeds our own in Los Angeles. But there, for example, I have ministered God's Word simply and without sensation for the past 20 years. Beginning with fewer than 30 believers, our constituency today numbers above 10,000. During these years we've seen 30,000 decisions for Christ, dozens of churches planted, and scores of workers sent to preach the gospel around the world. Again I assert, my testimony is *not* exceptional. Such reports of healings and miracles and church growth have become common worldwide, especially in the last 15 years.

THE LAUSANNE COVENANT

In this fifteenth year of the Lausanne movement, I am one with you, as together we watch the Holy Spirit's works of power spreading throughout the church. As at no other time in history, church growth is increasing at an exponential rate, as God's Word is being confirmed by the manifestation of the Holy Spirit's gifts. Though an enormous unfinished task is still before us, faith for its completion is rising.

In 1974, the first Lausanne Congress made a bold declaration concerning the ministry of the Holy Spirit. We have just heard it reread. In speaking for so broad a group of evangelicals, it was unlike any such statement before, including these words:

> We therefore call upon all Christians to pray for such a visitation of the sovereign Spirit of God that *all* his fruit may appear in *all* his people and that *all* his gifts may enrich the Body of Christ. *Only then* will the whole church become a fit instrument in his hands, that the whole earth may hear his voice.[2]

In the light of what has happened in the past fifteen years, who can estimate the degree to which the Lausanne Covenant has been *key* in welcoming a release of the Holy Spirit's power across the earth? To my perspective, the words of that Covenant have opened a door for multitudes of leaders:

- *First*: A doorway to investigating the Word of God and its *present promise* of power, with signs and wonders;
- *Second*: A doorway to *broadening fellowship*, overcoming fears and dissolving stereotypes which hinder boldness in faith and also sometimes divide brethren from one another; and, most of all,
- *Third*: I wonder if that 1974 Covenant may have uniquely opened a doorway to God Almighty Himself—to our *giving His Spirit license* to move freely in our midst, unshackled by the restraints of our—of my!—doubt and unbelief.

If a new passion for the Holy Spirit's works of power has begun a good work, how might it be more broadly advanced?

I propose three steps:

I. *First*, that we affirm the biblical base of our expecting the sign-gift ministry of the Holy Spirit today.

The Book of Acts begins, "The former treatise I have written, O Theophilus, of all that Jesus began to *do* and *teach*" (Acts 1:1). Luke's opening words assert that the church's work was and is to be a direct continuation of *all* Jesus' ministry. The text declares that the *actions* (what Jesus began to *do*) are as essential to the church's mission as the *proclamations* (what Jesus began to *teach*).

That Jesus' ministry was *both* a teaching/preaching ministry and a miracle/healing ministry is clear. For example:

Matthew 4:23-25—

Now Jesus went about all Galilee, teaching in their synagogues, preaching the gospel of the kingdom . . . (that's

what Jesus began to *teach* . . . then follows what Jesus also
did . . .) and healing all kinds of sickness . . . and those who
were demon-possessed, epileptics and paralytics; and He
healed them . . . .

So, the Book of Acts projects the church's ministry as *continuing* Jesus' ministry, a ministry defined in Jesus' words: "The works
that I do you shall do . . . and greater" (John 14:12).

The New Testament gives no reason for any hesitation to
expect supernatural signs of Jesus at work in my ministry. In fact,
candor with the Word of God holds me accountable today to
allow Jesus to do through *my* ministry the kinds of things He did
in *His*. In whatever part of His church He places me, it behooves
me to seek this balance: *to declare* the Word of God's love in Christ
and *to welcome* the Holy Spirit's works of power as well.

Beloved brethren and sisters, today's world need calls for no
less power than He displayed in the first century. As God's eternal
Word is confirmed by the Holy Spirit's supernatural power and
acts, we can expect new dimensions of triumph:

(a) *As at Ephesus*, New Age idolatry and satanism will be
exposed and overthrown;
(b) *As at Philippi*, demonic principalities controlling urban
centers will be cast down; and,
(c) *As at Mars Hill*, the barrenness of campus intellectualism
will be displayed.

Signs, wonders and miracles can shake Muslim peoples awake to
the superior power and claims of Jesus Christ. They can break
through the welter of human pain and tragedy with hope and healing.
And let us ask if Jesus wants to touch *today's* lepers with salvation and
healing. A global AIDS epidemic awaits the answer to that question.
Surely Jesus wants to heal the hopeless today just as He did long ago.

May I assure you, not *all* miracle ministry is automatically valid
or trustworthy! But beyond whatever shallowness or error I may
think present in some who practice a healing ministry, *I* need to

face these two facts—*the Word of God* and *a world of need. Both* call
me to a *personal passion for fullness* to answer the *human passion for
wholeness.* A balanced ministry is possible, and more and more are
hungering for Christ's fullness at *every* dimension.

How can this be?

The answer: to experience Christ's continuing *ministry,* we
need Christ's continuing *power.*

The *call* for Jesus' *fullest* ministry includes a *promise* by which
His power may be received. Jesus said, "You shall be baptized with
the Holy Spirit . . . and you shall receive power" (Acts 1:5, 8).
Whatever "the baptism with the Spirit" may mean to us, *whenever*
we may feel it is experienced, or *however* it may be evidenced, this
much is sure: Jesus said *that baptism* is to provide us with power to
minister everything Jesus has and is to the world He *died to redeem*
and *touch* with His fullness.

It is both inappropriate and unnecessary to debate theological
differences. These are essentially immaterial in the light of this
larger question I must answer: "Is the *power* of God's Spirit as evi-
dent in my *works* as the *truth* of God's Spirit is in my words?" *No*
structure or belief should block my passion for *all of Jesus* in *all of
my ministry.* That passion for fullness will open me to the Holy
Spirit's constant overflow in my life, welcoming His gifts and tran-
scending my limits with His almightiness.

Before his death, in his book, *Joy Unspeakable,* Martyn Lloyd-
Jones pled a case for each believer to be baptized in the Holy
Spirit as a distinct experience. He concludes by saying:

> May God give us all grace in this matter. It is not a matter
> for controversy, nor for proving who is right and who is wrong.
> The issue before us is the state of the Christian church, her
> weakness, her lethargy, with a world on fire, a world going to
> hell. We are the body of Christ but what do we need? The
> power! The pentecostal power! Shall we not with one accord,
> wait upon him and pray that again he may open the windows
> of heaven and shower down upon us the Holy Spirit in mighty
> reviving power? . . . The need today is for an authentication of

God, of the supernatural, of the spiritual, of the eternal, and
this can only be answered by God graciously hearing our cry
and shedding forth again his Spirit upon us and filling us as he
kept filling the early church.[3]

It is clear that the first church felt no need to argue when or
where they had *been* filled with the Spirit. For them, the issue was
being filled—*this* moment; for God's immediate purposes to be
served by the Spirit's present surge of supernatural power.

For example, when Paul confronts Elymas, whose demonic
control over the regional governor parallels barricades we face
today in cities and nations, the Bible says he was "filled with the
Holy Spirit" (Acts 13:9). In the fresh anointing of that moment,
Paul moves in miracle power to confound the works of hell and
advance the purposes of God.

However our various traditions interpret Jesus' words, "You
shall be baptized with the Holy Spirit . . . and you shall receive
power," to mean *let none of us* be satisfied with only a theological
position. My doctrinal precision is no substitute for the Holy
Spirit's demonstration. Paul's words call us all to affirm our
willingness to take the Bible-centered path to fullness, that we may
say, "My speech and my preaching were not with persuasive words
of human wisdom, but in demonstration of the Spirit and of
power, that your faith should not be in the wisdom of men but in
the power of God" (1 Corinthians 2:4, 5).

II. A *second* step toward realizing the Spirit's power in fullest
dimensions today is to acknowledge the fruit His signs and
wonders are already bringing.

Recent research reports abounding church growth is occurring
where the Holy Spirit's power works are revealing the fullness of
Christ through the church.

David Barrett's monumental work as the editor of the *World
Christian Encyclopedia* has provided us all with a broader perspective on the church's world witness.[4] Objective analysis of this
report requires the honest observation that the widest growth in

evangelism in most areas *regularly* correlates with the welcoming of the Holy Spirit's ministry of the supernatural—through His gifts, with signs and wonders.

An incredible harvest is being gathered.

Barrett's study records good growth anywhere evangelistic vigor is alive, but it also notes "many situations of *explosive, uncontrollable* growth," where the Holy Spirit's gifts are allowed and where signs and wonders confirm the Word.[5]

Evangelism has swelled the ranks of this segment of the Christian community, which in 1900 represented only seven-tenths of one percent of all Christians on the earth. Barrett reports these now involve almost one of every five Christians alive today.[6]

However, and of real concern, another researcher notes that a general unawareness of this phenomenal growth still exists where some prominent evangelical journals seem to ignore the impact of these ministries.[7] Why might this be, that *any* should hesitate to receive this report or rejoice in it? I suggest this reticence is provoked by prevailing and perfectly understandable fears.

Two kinds of "fear" seem to relate to the Holy Spirit's super-natural works; especially in regard to signs, wonders and the gifts. I understand them both, having grappled with them myself.

The first is *fear of the unfamiliar.*

I remember the first time I ever swam in a river. Until then, as a boy, I had only been in public swimming pools; but now, I suddenly found myself caught up in a slow but mighty stream, which was relentlessly carrying me beyond my entry point in the water. It was a new and unforgettably frightening sensation. In much the same way, first contacts with the miraculous dynamics of the Holy Spirit can be very disconcerting. When demons are confronted; where spiritual gifts are being manifest, which before were only verbal ideas; or where other unpredictable, surprising signs of God's holy power occur—first-time fears are understandable.

Second is an even more problematic fear: *the fear of fanaticism.* It is justifiable that anyone fears the risk of fanaticism where the Spirit's mighty works are present.

There have been excesses.

But fairness will see that the excesses are more due to human idiosyncrasy (style) than arguments against the validity of supernatural ministry. Sensationalism and exploitation have always been a problem; Peter faced that long ago. But in rebuking Simon the Sorcerer he provides us with a challenging model. Could the Holy Spirit be calling us today to exercise the choice Peter did then—to sort the chaff from the wheat, to expose the serpent and release the dove?

As a Christian leader, it is worth my determination to gain an acquaintance with the supernatural operations and manifestations of the Holy Spirit. I *can't* free Him to work mightily without risking my loss of control in some situations. But I *can* learn to *trust* Him, and learn how to move with His power in a way that restrains foolishness, sustains *His* control and still releases fullness. Let me appeal to every mature, Bible-centered leader: Let us open ourselves to the broadest movings of the Holy Spirit, for He's clearly ready to bring broader advances in evangelizing every nation. If we all *will* open to Him, two tragedies can be avoided:

(1) Ministry in the gifts of the Spirit with signs and wonders will be shaped by leaders who prioritize biblical values, *rather than* be forfeited to the few who may seem indifferent to those priorities; and

(2) We shall *all* be equipped throughout *all* the Church to reach to *all* the world with *all* the resources Jesus promised; *rather than* attempting to pursue *all* the task without *all* the power He commanded us *all* to receive.

Surely we *all* feel a passion for fullness!

III. So as a *third* step toward satisfying that passion, *let us affirm a united quest.*

Paul Cedar is a friend of mine.

He is pastor of Lake Avenue Congregational Church in Pasadena, California, and a member of the Lausanne Committee. Paul recently said to me, "Jack, I want to find a word that describes us both. We both want all the power, gifts and miracles the Holy

Spirit has to give, and I don't like people putting us in separate pockets because you're Pentecostal and I'm not."

I think he's addressed an important point on the subject of the Holy Spirit's Power in Evangelism. Why? Because as long as we allow sectarian titles or stereotypes to block our personally answering the Spirit's call to the fullness of Christ's ministry, too many of us will forego something of God's pure power in our ministry. Christ's prayer for our unity, "that the world may know," is not His mandate to our total doctrinal agreement any more than to our uniformity in church government. But He *is* calling us all to acknowledge His *fullness*—to be people with a passion for "all the fullness of God"; people who *all* are *candidates* to *minister* in the power, gifts and grace of the Holy Spirit.

May I submit a definition of Spirit-filled ministry?

I propose that a Spirit-filled ministry is one characterized by all that Jesus *is*, all that Jesus *does*, and all that Jesus *wants*. Spirit-filled ministry is Christ-filled ministry, when *Christ*, the *Anointed King*, is manifest *in and through* us by the anointing of the Holy Spirit.

His is an "anointing" which *enables, ensures* and *enlarges*:

(a)   The Spirit *enables* the believer for service and witness, giving *gifts* which focus on answering human need, not personal, selfish or private interests; gifts that bear witness to the faithful Word, exalting Christ and the triumph of His Cross as signs and wonders confirm His Resurrection rule and power.

(b)   The Spirit *ensures* the uniqueness of each personality. He doesn't violate the Father's handiwork by forcing any of us into a stereotyped method of ministering in the Holy Spirit's gifts and power. He'll use each of us in different ways—even when exercising the same gifts.

(c)   The Spirit will *enlarge* our heart and vision. He will make us more *like* Jesus and make us *love* all who are His. He will deal a deathblow to sectarian smallness and help us all understand the vastness and difference of the many members who form His body.

In Paul's prayer "that you may be filled with all the fullness of God," *pleroma* is the word translated "fullness." It means *"the full content, entirety and whole sum"* and is most often used in reference to the Person of Christ Jesus Himself![8]

Perhaps *pleroma* is the word for a new era in evangelism.

Could it be, as we stand on the threshold of the twenty-first century, that this is the word—the *ministry*—He would give us; ministry that breaks through in *all* Christ's fullness and power as we are filled and energized by the Holy Spirit?

What will result?

The result will be a *fullness in worship, a fullness in the Word, a fullness in integrity and character, a fullness in serving the poor, a fullness in loving one another, a fullness in lay involvement* and *a fullness in the Spirit* with power, gifts, signs and wonders enhancing a *fullness in evangelism.* Then we'll be able to say with Paul, "And when I come to you, I shall come in—*pleroma*—the fullness of the blessing of the gospel of Christ."

That fullness brings breakthrough, because it declares the word of the Cross and the glory of Christ; because it confronts demonic powers in the power of the Blood of the Lamb and in the spirit of prayer; and because it is attended by signs and wonders as the Lord confirms His Word with signs following.

That's the heritage of the people of the *pleroma*: the fullness of Christ. Their ministry is filled with the Holy Spirit and His power.

They preach the Word, but they're more than biblical;

They baptize their converts, but they're more than Baptist;

They govern their congregations in distinct ways, but they're more than Free Church, Presbyterian, Episcopalian or Congregational.

They may speak with tongues, but they're more than Pentecostal.

They function in the Spirit's gifts, but they're more than Charismatic.

They flow in the Spirit's power, but they're more than Third Wave.

What might we *all* be called as we all welcome a fresh fullness of the Holy Spirit's power to equip us for evangelism?

Since we would be people of the *pleroma*—the fullness—we might be called *pleromatics*; that is, people committed to witness to *all* God's Word with *all* the Spirit's wonders, until *all* the world is reached with *all* Christ's fullness! Or, we might be called believers, saints or disciples. But perhaps, we might best simply live together under the name given us long ago. When Holy Spirit-filled people first shook an entire pagan city through God's miracle grace and power, "They were first called Christians at Antioch."

Christians! Because *Christ* is Jesus' title as the Anointed One who ministered in the fullness of the Spirit's power, so, *Christian* is the right name for people whose passion is to continue in that anointing.

So, dear ones in Christ—let us give *full* acknowledgment to the *biblical* basis for our call to continue Jesus' ministry, *both* in the Word of truth and in the Spirit of power. Let us *accept* and *rejoice* in the evidence that such fullness of ministry is available and abounding today.

And let us, with one heart, affirm our passion for that Christ-like fullness answering anew the call of the Lausanne Covenant, to "pray for such a visitation of the sovereign Spirit of God that all His fruit may appear in all His people and that all His gifts may enrich the body of Christ"; because we agree that "only then will the whole Church become a fit instrument in His hands, that the whole earth may hear His voice." *Amen.*

*   *   *   *   *

The message was acknowledged with applause warm enough to indicate that what had been said was received by far more than the minority percentage of the Congress representing the Pentecostal/charismatic community. Then I moved directly ahead, reminding the assembly of my assignment to continue now—to lead them in a season of worship and prayer as we together responded to the messages of the evening.

CHAPTER

3

"When is the last time you did anything
for the first time for Jesus' sake?"

Deciding to Give
Place to God

As we began to sing, "Spirit of the Living God, fall afresh on me," I encouraged all to open their hearts with childlikeness and simplicity—to humble ourselves before God. There was an immediate swell of heartfelt prayer.

People were standing everywhere, many extending their hands in earnest—indeed, passionate—prayer and praise. The huge hall was pulsating with genuine emotion as a holy intensity rose to dominate the moment. Clearly there was more than a casual stance of soul among vast numbers of the assembly. I was simply standing at the pulpit, praying quietly—seeking to be careful *not* to say or do anything which I thought might offend anyone in the broadly representative audience. Later, I would discover that a small number of those present were, at that moment, afraid of some "takeover," as though an emotionalistic binge were imminent. Some would accuse me of pressuring the situation. But having led thousands of openly expressive prayer and worship services in my life, I not only knew the genuineness of what was occurring, I also felt responsible to a special sensitivity.

Realizing the scope of the representation here, and knowing many were unaccustomed to a demonstrative response of *any* kind, I wanted no one to feel that anything I did was intended to coerce or manipulate such a response. Thus, I exercised a deliberate restraint in the volume of my prayer and the stance of my posture. Nonetheless, without promotion—only release—prolonged praise with impassioned prayer filled the room as thousands together invited the Holy Spirit of God to freshly engulf us, our lives and our ministries. Because I had sought to be sensitive, it was bewildering the next day to be asked why I had sought to impose a sectarian style of prayer and praise on the Congress. That question in no wise represented a majority of the participants, but I felt troubled that it represented any at all. I was reminded again of my own past fears of opening to God's power—fearing that to surrender control to Him was tantamount to denying intelligence or coherency and stumbling into mouth-frothing idiocy!

The few protests raised (which were graciously and tactfully handled by the Congress leadership) reflect a very human inclination in many of us. How many of us have wrestled with that very real, internal sense of restraint generated by our fear of being "controlled by God," or worse yet, of "losing control"? Our emotions are reined in (banded with a steel-like resistance to "emotionalism") as we become blind to the emotion forcing our rigidity—fear. Further, this fear-filled stance is then reinforced by our suppositions that God deals primarily with our intellect—as though our minds were the substance of our beings. How often it fails to occur to us that not only was God equally pleased to create our emotions as well as our mind, but He also willingly deals with us at both levels. Should we not recant our fears, confessing that to suppress *either* is to violate trust toward Him?

Look at an inverse illustration of the point, when *intellect* is refused a fair place. Consider the unbeliever you have met who scoffs at your Christian faith. Belief in the Resurrection is mocked and the person of Christ reduced to, at best, a humanistic representation of the divine nature of Jesus. Notwithstanding the abundance of outstanding writings which give a reasoned, intellectually satisfying case for vital faith, millions refuse to bother with reading even the briefest presentation of the facts. Steeling their minds, they shun exposure to even the most basic historic or scientific evidence for believing in the authenticity of the Bible, the Person of Jesus Christ and His confirming Resurrection. The truth is that they are afraid of faith—afraid to open their minds to the possibility that to give God space in their minds may cost them giving Him more than they want. The mind is neutralized to preempt God's entry. So it is, by analogy, that this same neutralization is no less present when believers in Christ fear giving place to the Holy Spirit's dealings with their emotions. Just as the unbeliever is warned, "Don't let them brainwash you," so, as a believer, I've been told, "Watch out for emotionalism."

Some years ago I began to disbelieve those who, while not saying as much, still demonstrated by their actions their belief that *any* allowance of emotional expression was a sure pathway to mindless faith, if not whooping fanaticism. It began to dawn on me that, given an environment where the Word of God was *foundational* and the Person of Christ the *focus*, the Holy Spirit could be trusted to do *both*—enlighten the intelligence and ignite the emotions. I soon discovered that to allow Him that much space necessitates more a surrender of my senseless fears than a surrender of sensible control. God is not asking any of us to abandon reason or succumb to some euphoric feeling. He is, however, calling us to trust Him—enough to give *Him* control.

On the occasion in Manila, I was amazed to discover the next day that some people were irritated for the simplest of reasons: (1) I had at one point during the extended season of prayer invited leaders to form small groups of three or four in circles of shared prayer—together acknowledging our need for more of God's fullness in our ministries; (2) I had, at another time, invited all in the Congress hall to join hands, forming a single band of prayer across the breadth of the huge auditorium; (3) I had, in teaching a simple song of prayer, suggested each person touch his or her own ears, eyes, lips and heart at the appropriate time as we sang,

"Holy Spirit come, make my ears to hear;
Make my eyes to see, make my lips to speak,
Make my heart to seek and my hands to reach out
And touch the world with Your love."

Peculiarly, these actions were deemed "manipulative," even
though they were only means of inviting united prayer in
welcoming the Holy Spirit. The truth is, the issue was neither
manipulation nor emotionalism—the issue was fear: fear of being
stretched or fear of "losing control."

We all face it! And we've all been schooled in enough systems
of rhetoric or resistance to withstand the tender dealings of God,
who has pointedly said He seeks for childlike hearts and
responsive souls. Such "responsive souls" are certainly not without
minds—but neither are they without *emotions*.

In the last analysis, an honest approach to the Bible and to
church history confronts us with this fact: the unwillingness to
have our emotions impacted leads us to limiting God's workings in
our whole being, life, service and witness.

- Abraham's grandest moment is as emotionally laden as any
  in history. "Take your son, your only son Isaac, and offer
  him." Any suggestion that *that* episode was without
  emotion is intellectually vacuous!
- Jacob's breakthrough in prayer, resulting in his being
  renamed "Israel" and setting him forward to realize his
  God-intended destiny, comes after a night-long wrestling
  match. That's *passion*—and look at the purposeful results.
- David's dancing praise, Isaiah's prostrated "Woe!" Daniel's
  three-week fast, Hosea's broken heart, Jesus' anger with the
  Pharisees, Pentecost's praise meeting which evoked
  accusations of drunkenness—all are sanctified emotions!

One runs the risk of seeming to argue for emotionalism.
However, the "ism" on any matter is born when the thing is sought
for its own sake: when intellect becomes intellectu*alism* or

denomination becomes denominational*ism*; when a proper thing becomes sought for its value *alone* at the expense of other values. But my plea that we allow God to have space to work in our whole soul—mind *and* emotions—is not a plea for emotional*ism*. It is only a healthy request for our yielding permission for our *passions* to be aflame as truly as we allow our *perception* to be alert.

The testimony of history is as convincing as the evidence of Scripture. The brilliance of John Wesley's mind, schooled to a fine edge, was coupled with a devotion to duty that took him from England to the primitive setting of missionary work in early Georgia. Still, he perceived an emptiness in his soul, which was unchanged until his famous "heartwarming" experience. That experience points up two practical values for any who hesitate before "emotions":

1. His emotional response to a reasoned discourse on the Book of Romans evidences that his intellect was not unemployed at the time. *Point*: Spiritually based *passion* is born of biblically based perception.

2. His ready acknowledgment that his emotions were significant to the moment evidences that a great mind was not ashamed to humbly describe its limits. "Strangely warmed" are measured words lodged in the emotionally economic speech of an era when "feelings" were every bit as suspect as today. Yet Wesley's future hinged on that response, and it was real and decisive. *Point*: Decisions which determine our destiny will never be made in an emotional vacuum.

FINNEY'S TESTIMONY

Other notables of relatively recent church history speak to us of the validity and propriety of deep, impassioned encounters with God. Charles Finney and Dwight L. Moody each recorded such experiences. As we read their reports of profound emotional experiences, are we not wise to realize that these brilliant leaders must have had some motive in leaving such records for posterity? They obviously did not retell their private experiences in a cheap attempt to impress people, and they were clearly above employing sensational devices to prod their people toward emotionalism. But knowing how pivotal these events were in their lives, they recorded them—with a ready will to expose their souls—to explain their own *passion*. They not only knew their own essential need for the experiences they retell, but they submitted the retelling because they knew the value of each Christian being brought to such a moment—the moment he decides to give place to God.

Finney's testimony is of marked significance because of the remarkable intellect of the man. His theological writings are the product of a mind alert, alive and aglow. Yet in his own words, he describes the personal breakthrough in his own experience, in which the Holy Spirit swept over him in baptizing power.

V. Raymond Edman, the beloved missionary who concluded his many fruitful years of ministry in serving as President of Wheaton College, quotes Finney's own report in his book, *They Found the Secret*.[1] Returning one day from an interview, Finney entered his office, and without any preliminary expectation that such a moment should seize him, he remembers: "As I turned and was about to take a seat by the fire, I received a mighty baptism of the Holy Ghost.

"The Holy Spirit descended upon me in a manner that seemed to go through me, body and soul. I could feel the impression, like a wave of electricity, going through and through me. Indeed, it seemed to come in waves and waves of liquid love; for I could not express it in any other way. It seemed like the very breath of God. I can recollect distinctly that it seemed to fan me, like immense wings.

"No words can express the wonderful love that was shed abroad in my heart. I wept aloud with joy and love; and I do not know but I should say, I literally bellowed out the unutterable gushing of my heart.

"These waves came over me, and over me, and over me, one after the other, until I recollect I cried out, 'I shall die if these waves continue to pass over me.' I said, 'Lord, I cannot bear any more'; yet I had no fear of death.

"How long I continued in this state, with this baptism continuing to roll over me and go through me, I do not know. But I know it was late in the evening when a member of my choir—for I was the leader of the choir—came into the office to see me. He was a member of the church. He found me in this state of loud weeping, and said to me, 'Mr. Finney, what ails you?' I could make him no answer for some time. He then said, 'Are you in pain?' I gathered myself up as best I could, and replied, 'No, but so happy that I cannot live . . . .,

"I soon fell asleep, but almost as soon awoke again on account of the great flow of the love of God that was in my heart. I was so filled with love that I could not sleep. Soon I fell asleep again, and awoke in the same manner. When I awoke, this temptation would return upon me, and the love that seemed to be in my heart would abate; but as soon as I was asleep, it was so warm within me that I would immediately awake. Thus I continued till, late at night, I obtained some sound repose.

"When I awoke in the morning the sun had risen, and was pouring a clear light into my room. Words cannot express the impression that this sunlight made upon me. Instantly the baptism that I had received the night before returned upon me in the same manner. I arose upon my knees in the bed and wept aloud with joy, and remained for some time too much overwhelmed with the baptism of the Spirit to do anything but pour out my soul to God. It seemed as if this morning's baptism was accompanied with a gentle reproof, and the Spirit seemed to say to me, 'Will you doubt? Will you doubt?' I cried, 'No! I will not doubt; I cannot doubt.' He then cleared the subject up so much to my mind that it was in fact impossible for me to doubt that the Spirit of God had taken possession of my soul."

There is no way to reread this journal entry of so mighty a man of God and allow ourselves lightly to set aside the possibility of our own need for such a stark, stirring and staggering encounter. Being open to that possibility is not to propose a quest for a precise replica of Finney's experience. The Holy Spirit will come to each of us in unique and personal ways, for He is never stereotypical in His dealings. However, to tolerate any disposition I may have to hold Him at bay by an unwillingness to be shaken to the core of my being, would be as dishonest with God as if I were to insist He visit me in exactly the same way as He has another. The quest for a repeat performance by the Almighty is as presumptuous as to request a restrained one. My call for God to visit me only requires *passion*, not prescriptions. He's the Doctor, and He alone knows what I need of His manifestations to remedy my reserve, deliver me from pride and crush the fruit of His grace within me until it flows with the vibrancy of new wine.

MOODY'S "FILLING"

Dwight L. Moody's influence continues to bless the whole body of Christ a full century after his height of ministry. The Moody Church in Chicago, Moody Bible Institute, the Moody Radio Network and Moody Press, all are a continued outflowing of a river of mightiness that began in the soul of this one man—passionate for God. He describes the pathway by which he came to his own "anointing" or "filling" (his words) with the Holy Spirit.

He had begun to be awakened to his need through a brief, momentary contact with an aged man whom he met one day following a service in New York. The gray-haired saint touched Moody's shoulder and, as the evangelist turned to look into his eyes, spoke these earnest, pointed words: "Young man, when you speak again, honor the Holy Ghost." Moody elaborates this poignant dealing of the Lord, linking it to the prayers and personal words of encouragement he received from two godly women in his congregation. They had gently spoken to him of their praying for his "anointing for special service."

"You need power," they urged their pastor, yet not without respect.

Moody confides his inner thoughts at the time.

"I need power?" I said to myself. "Why, I thought I had power. I had a large Sabbath school, and the largest congregation in Chicago. There were *some* conversions at the time, and I was in a sense satisfied."

He describes the awakening of his own passion for fullness. "There came a great hunger into my soul. I knew not what it was. I began to cry as never before. The hunger increased. I really felt that I did not want to live any longer if I could not have this power for service. I kept on crying all the time that God would fill me with His Spirit."

While in New York, seeking help for victims of the great Chicago fire of 1871, which destroyed a third of the city, Moody's quest was answered. He says:

My heart was not in the work of begging. I could not appeal. I was crying all the time that God would fill me with His Spirit. Well, one day, in the city of New York—oh, what a day!—I cannot describe it. I seldom refer to it; it is almost too sacred an experience to name. Paul had an experience of which he didn't speak for fourteen years. I can only say that God revealed Himself to me, and I had such an experience of His love that I had to ask Him to stay His hand.

I went to preaching again. The sermons were not different; I did not present any new truths, and yet hundreds were converted. I would not now be placed back where I was before that blessed experience if you should give me all the world—it would be as the small dust of the balance.[2]

The common denominator of each of these testimonies is that *intelligent* men became *passionate* for God and that each experienced an encounter with Him that went *beyond* mere emotions. But they *made no apology for including emotions.*

Is there a way to reinstate the emotions to a place of respect as a human response, unsuspected by sincere believers? What truly great goal has ever been sought merely on the basis of analysis? What human pain or need has ever been addressed simply on the basis of empirical evidence? What initial commitment to sacrifice and self-giving has been born without the throes and thrill of patriotism, devotion, affection or a heart-stirring ideal? What true humiliation of soul has ever been acknowledged apart from the emotional grip of guilt, inadequacy or helplessness before human need?

The Bible is without apology in declaring that Jesus, "for the joy that was set before Him, endured the cross, despising the shame . . ." (Hebrews 12:2). The power of one emotion overthrew the power of another—joy overcame shame.

Calvary was a reasoned, predetermined plan in the Father's counsels, and agreed to before all worlds by the Son, who knew He would become the sacrificial Lamb. In intellectual terms, it was all settled. But at Gethsemane, passion rises and blood-sweat oozes from the pores of the God-man who is caught in the welter of the emotion and tension of actualizing the redemptive plan.

There is the point.

When we discuss the issue of *passion* for Holy Spirit fullness, we are discussing the advancing of the message and ministry of the Lamb's redemptive provision! What burst upon the lips of thousands in Manila was more than a superficial quest for a transient spasm of spiritual ecstasy. The issue was *passion* and it continues to be the issue in every era of the church. For some the only concern is that emotions be carefully controlled to the point of their atrophying. But as we prayed together at Lausanne II, the focus was global evangelism—for being fully equipped with the Holy Spirit's power for the task. The point wasn't "feelings"; the point was—and *is!*—becoming concerned enough about being filled with God to forsake the calmness of our ordinary behavior and to seek hard after Him—with all our hearts!

Further, this passion is for more than one facet of God's grace and working. The passion for fullness is a quest for the multifaceted operations of God's truth and power to be realized in beauty and balance, then to explode upon the darkness in which hell seeks to veil mankind. The light that shatters that gloom is not from some blissful star glowing over Bethlehem, but from blazing tongues burning over the heads of the 120 at Pentecost.

Indeed, there is a beauty and balance to the whole of His Word and His way, but it will never be realized dispassionately.

A purely intellectual or theological exercise will never obtain "all the fullness of God." It isn't something we reason toward, but something we hunger for.

Many have written me (and some journals have expressed the same sentiment) that Manila was a milestone, and that the evening in which we focused on the Holy Spirit's ministry was a moment of crucial significance. Their words and my viewpoint on that possibility are completely apart from my involvement in the event. I am neither so stupid nor so vain as to suppose that either my or James Packer's message determined the moment, for I believe the moment was *pre*determined! It takes little discernment to recognize the Holy Spirit is moving at the Father's will and in His sovereign timing to awaken, to rekindle and to unite the church for mighty, earth-shaking evangelistic enterprises in our day.

To weld the Body as one, "that the world may know," will require a combination of both passion and perception. Much of what follows deals with perceptions of and perspectives on God's Word as it relates to spiritually ignited life and service. But before we proceed to that, we had best settle the question as to how passionate we are willing to become. How vulnerable will I allow myself to be? How available to a holy upheaval in my soul—including my emotions?

The Father's kingdom order is simple and clear. There is no satisfaction unpreceded by deep hunger and driving thirst. There is no birth without travail, nor any kingdom breakthrough without a violence that seizes it by force.

We must settle the issue of passion first.

Not the passion of an emotional pursuit, but the passion for a work of God in our day which *exceeds* our best-laid plans, *expands* our shrunken hearts, *extends* our withered reach and *exalts* Jesus in our minds—until we have no reasons left to resist His Spirit's mightiness changing our lives and supercharging our witness.

To allow the awakening of such passion in us puts us in a historic line of men and women who hear God's heart, take His hand and learn His ways.

"Abraham's seed" is their generic name. In *each* generation each of them *re*learn, through their *own* pursuit, what every generation has learned since that founder of the faith-walk learned it for himself. No one automatically inherits the experience of faith's dynamic, only its promise. The promise is secure in God's oath, but its dynamism is only released as each partakes of it. Abraham learned that for himself and so must we today.

That's always been true—even with the very first generation following Abraham's footsteps.

Isaac.

CHAPTER

4

For whatever things were written before were written for our learning, that we through the patience and comfort of the Scriptures might have hope. Romans 15:4

Redigging the Wells

He squinted his eyes, narrowing them against the glare of the midday sun. He licked his lips then quickly dried them on his sleeve. His measuring gaze told him he would be at the well within the hour. The arid heat of the Arabah was welcomed by the hiker's aging body, warming the muscles and relaxing his gait as he strode toward the finish of what had been a long morning's walk with God.

Isaac had risen early, sensing something of the same summons he had felt on other occasions when Yahweh had met him—had spoken in distinct and special ways. Now, on this day, the sense of this Companion's presence was no less, but no words had been spoken—simply a survey had been made. Together, they had walked the paths which networked the wells belonging to this man.

The wells of Isaac, he thought, *the son of Abraham.*

Finally, as he sat beneath the palms at Rehoboth, he

completed his summary of the history of these wells. He knew the significance of this exercise: "Yahweh wants this story relayed to my offspring." It was the reason for this morningtime journey with God, and Isaac sensed his assignment to frame the story in the form and cadence of those oral renditions of other events in which the history of his family was retained.

It had begun with the Almighty's charge, years before: "Sojourn in this land, and I will be with you and bless you; for to you and your descendants I give all these lands, and I will perform the oath which I swore to Abraham your father" (Genesis 26:3).

The covenant. It had always been a mystery to Isaac.

Since the first time he had heard his father speak of it, he had been impressed with its scope. The foundational promise of offspring and property possessions was assuring, as Yahweh guaranteed the blessings of children and land upon which to raise them. Both seemed very logical and very desirable—not unlike what any man would hope that God would grant him.

But Abraham had told him that this covenant involved much more.

"My son, you must always remember, our God not only has promised us blessing, but He has chosen us to *be* a blessing also, a people through whom He will bless multitudes—even all the peoples of the earth."

These words had been riveted in Isaac's consciousness as the result of another occasion with his father. They had traveled to Moriah—the mountain to the north. Yahweh had called Abraham there to offer a sacrifice. It was unforgettable. It was unforgettable first, because of his discovery that he was to be the sacrifice! But beyond that, the deepest recollection which registered sweet remembrance in his soul was how an incredible confidence had come upon him. The unexplainable peace could only be accounted for in one way. Yahweh. The powerful presence of God had surrounded them both.

He had not been afraid.

There was no way to describe it adequately. While carrying the wood up the hill, it had begun to dawn on his awareness that he was the intended sacrifice; yet he had felt nothing but a will to submit to this mysterious thing that was happening.

And then the ram was in the bushes—trapped and tangled by its horns. And his father halted—knife raised over his head. Later he would tell Isaac how, in that instant, Yahweh had spoken and said to substitute the ram for his son as the sacrifice.

The memory of that experience had never left him. He knew he was a chosen instrument of the Lord, spared for the purposes of the God of all the heavens and the earth. Just as his father before him, he was selected to be a conduit of blessing to future generations and to every people and nation.

The tinkling of sheep bells caught his ear. Rising from his resting place near the well, he returned the stone vessel from which he had drunk to its nesting place in the crotch of an upcropping of rocks above the mouth of the well. Stepping upon the rocks for advantage in viewing, he caught the eye of the advancing shepherds moving toward the well with their flock.

"Ho! My lord!" called Elihu.

They were all his men and these were his flocks, as was the surrounding countryside as far as the eye could see. But it had not always been so, and Elihu, who had quickened his pace toward the well to greet his master, knew the story as well as any.

"What brings you here—is there trouble? Marauders?"

"No, Elihu. If you can believe this—I'm only out for a walk," Isaac laughed.

The grizzled features of the older shepherd cracked with a smile as he croaked out a chuckle, "A walk! Where is your next stop? Ararat?!"

They embraced after the tradition of their greeting, and as Elihu went to retrieve the stone vessel for his own use at refreshment, Isaac explained, "No, I'm not going that far, but it's strange you should mention *that* site."

Elihu's head tilted as he drank deeply, but his eyes remained on Isaac, inquiring without words. By now the other shepherds had begun grouping the sheep for relays at watering, deferring to the conversation between their foreman and their master, who had now moved to a shady resting place some distance from the well.

"Elihu, you know God's promise to Noah—and you have heard His promise to both my father and me. This past night, I have felt the strongest dealings of His hand—reminding me of His might and our struggles in obtaining this land and these wells. As I rose, He stirred my desire to retrace the paths between these watering holes for which you and I wrestled against adversaries in years now past.

"Yahweh has walked with me this day, constraining me to formalize the story of our struggle—of our passion in possessing this territory and redigging these wells. He has caused me to know it is of His mind and will to keep this memory for retelling in future generations.

"I feel it is His fortune that just as I have completed my circuit I have encountered you. Elihu, you were there with me—through it all. Let me review the account as it has come to my heart to tell it. See if there is anything to add or adjust."

And there, beside an ancient well nearly two thousand years before Christ, a man for the first time verbalized in ordered sequence the tale of his pursuit of God's promise to him. It would be transmitted to future generations in precisely these words:

> Then Isaac sowed in that land, and reaped in the same year a hundredfold; and the Lord blessed him. The man began to prosper, and continued prospering until he became very prosperous; for he had possessions of flocks and possessions of herds and a great number of servants. So the Philistines envied him. Now the Philistines had stopped up all the wells which his father's servants had dug in the days of Abraham his father, and they had filled them with earth. And Abimelech said to Isaac, "Go away from us, for you are much mightier than we."
>
> Then Isaac departed from there and pitched his tent in the Valley of Gerar, and dwelt there. And Isaac dug again the wells of water which they had dug in the days of Abraham his father, for the Philistines had stopped them up after the death of Abraham. He called them by the names which his father

had called them. Also Isaac's servants dug in the valley, and
found a well of running water there. But the herdsmen of
Gerar quarreled with Isaac's herdsmen, saying, "The water is
ours." So he called the name of the well Esek, because they
quarreled with him. Then they dug another well, and they
quarreled over that one also. So he called its name Sitnah. And
he moved from there and dug another well, and they did not
quarrel over it. So he called its name Rehoboth, because he
said, "For now the Lord has made room for us, and we shall be
fruitful in the land."

Then he went up from there to Beersheba. And the Lord
appeared to him the same night and said, "I am the God of
your father Abraham; do not fear, for I am with you. I will
bless you and multiply your descendants for My servant
Abraham's sake." So he built an altar there and called on the
name of the Lord, and he pitched his tent there; and there
Isaac's servants dug a well (Genesis 26:12-25).

The rise and fall of Isaac's voice ceased. His eyes, which during
the entirety of his recitation had been fixed on the haze-shrouded
mountains to the east, turned to rest on Elihu.

"Exactly," said the slightly older man. "It was as you have said.
The struggle was long, but it was worth it. And indeed, Yahweh
has been with us."

"Indeed and amen, dear friend," replied Isaac as he stood,
brushing the dust from his garment. "But one question remains
now, since you have confirmed the clarity and completeness of my
story."

"Which is?"

"What might it be that future generations shall face, Elihu,
that Yahweh has impressed me to prepare the story of our struggle
for their learning?"

*   *   *   *   *   *

The Bible is history, not legend, and its stories are to beget
faith, not merely repeat folklore. The story of Isaac's struggle to

obtain the wells, which would bring immediate promise and extend the covenanted purposes of God through him *and* his offspring, unfolds lessons for our application.

Isaac's is a story of passion in pursuit of plenty, recorded to remind people of God's covenant that the promise is only obtained where sufficient desire is present.

A half-dozen truths spill from this account, inviting us to review them for the very purpose God directed they be recorded in His Word: for our *learning*, our *patience*, our *comfort* and our *hope*. "For whatever things were written before were written for our learning, that we through the patience and comfort of the Scriptures might have hope" (Romans 15:4).

HERE IS LEARNING

The lessons from Isaac's struggle for the wells begin with a man who is (1) a child of promise and (2) a person of prosperity.

"I will make your descendants multiply as the stars of the heaven; I will give to your descendants all these lands; and in your seed all the nations of the earth shall be blessed . . . ."

"Then Isaac sowed . . . reaped . . . and the Lord blessed him . . . and continued prospering until he became very prosperous" (Genesis 26:4, 12, 13).

Blessing is always the beginning place of divine commission.

God never calls us to action or service without first having established grounds from which we may move. That is the "sovereign" side of all the issues of life. He gives *first* and He gives *most*. Whatever we are asked to respond with is always "afterward and less than," for He summons our faith after He has first displayed His faithfulness.

The story of Isaac's struggle begins with a man of whom it might be said, both in terms of faith as well as economics, "He was born with a silver spoon in his mouth." As inheritor of Abraham's covenant Isaac is also the sole possessor of Abraham's wealth.

Furthermore, the context reveals that like Abraham, even Isaac's foibles turn to fruitfulness. Seeking to escape famine conditions in one area he moves to another, and is stopped en route to Egypt by God's directive. The stopping place—in Gerar, Philistine country controlled by King Abimelech—provides the scene of a repeat performance of his father's self-protecting ruse: "Say you're my sister, dear. It will save my neck!" But instead of distancing him from Abimelech when the king discovers Isaac's dishonesty, the results are beneficial. Abimelech feels obligated to Isaac and issues a dictum in his favor.

The story simply smacks with the obvious; it is designed by God Himself to parade before our own eyes the message of His sovereign grace which besets us before and behind and overspreads and undergirds our lives. We deserve nothing, but we are inheritors of all; we stumble forward, kept all the while by His power and made fruitful in spite of ourselves! Grace is the fountainhead of all we are and the foundation of all we can become. But that lesson learned, it is our wisdom to see that grace has never been shown as an end in itself.

Grace is the footing upon which God calls us to build in faith.

PATIENCE—PURSUING PURPOSE

The test of Isaac's character is neither in his inheritance nor even in his moments of fear-for-self which prompted his deceiving Abimelech. It is in his reaction to the episodes involving the Philistines stopping of his wells—filling them with dirt and debris until they are useless for either refreshing or irrigation, not to mention survival. "Then Isaac departed . . . And Isaac dug again the wells of water which they had dug in the days of Abraham his father . . . He called them by the names which his father had called them" (Genesis 26:17, 18).

The essence of patience is how we bear up under the stress of circumstance that seeks to stifle God's purpose in our lives. Isaac's gentle-yet-militant response provides a balanced approach to our answering today's call to redig the wells our fathers have left.

Without belligerence, Isaac peacefully relocates at the jealous Philistines' behest, but at once asserts his will to see the wells flowing again.

There is nothing "silver-spooned" about this man! Whatever has been bequeathed to him in no way is presumed as "his due." The ensuing verses record one quarrel after another as Isaac contends to secure the wells essential to his realizing God's intended purposes for him. The naming of Esek (quarrel) and Sitnah (enmity) leaves the timeless reminder that the pathway to spacious fruitfulness (Rehoboth) will always be gained only through struggle.

COMFORT IN HIS PROMISE

Remarkably, Genesis 26 records *two* appearances of the Lord to Isaac. The first is the instance in which the covenant God made with Abraham is transmitted to Isaac. The word of the Lord projects *purpose*—and the struggle which followed gives evidence that Isaac took that purpose seriously, being neither passive nor apathetic when it was threatened by opponents.

Now in the latter part of the same passage, following Isaac's contending for the wells, the Lord visits him again: "I am the God of your father Abraham; do not fear, for I am with you. I will bless you and multiply your descendants for my servant Abraham's sake" (v.24).

Isaac immediately builds an altar there—the evidence that he has had his *own* confirmation of God's promise, not merely a relaying of his father's promise. And he digs another well on the spot.

This passage is pregnant with meaning. Truth is wrapped in the womb of this struggle-story to await periodic birthing in any who will allow the Holy Spirit to beget it in their own lives.

- We are all joint heirs of eternal salvation through Jesus Christ, the seed of Abraham.

- The Father's promise to His Son, that He shall inherit the nations, is transmitted to us as a shared promise.

- The sands of history in the hands of our adversaries have often choked the fountains of the lifeflow which is the secret to the church's fruitfulness.

- Where earnest souls pursue the original wells of blessing and power, God will not only reward their pursuit with refreshing, but He will confirm His Word to them anew—contemporarily, personally and with promised power.

It's enough to stir the sincere to the task of *redigging*, for the fountains of God's divine power—given to advance His divine purpose in us—are not at new and original places. They are right where they have always been: "All my springs are in You, . . . Deep calls unto deep at the noise of Your waterfalls" (Psalm 87:7; 42:7).

The passion for fullness is a passion for God Himself.

It is practical, for it is rooted in a tangible objective—the fulfillment of His purpose in our lives and the fruitfulness of His mission through our witness. This is no call to submerge the psyche in mystical Christianity. The Holy Spirit is drawing us to the living springs of God's own Person, that *there*—in the presence of Almighty mightiness and Ancient-of-Days timelessness—we might find the satisfying fountain of sufficiency and relevancy.

HOPE—PROMISED FULLNESS *NOW*

The deep thunderings of heaven's waterfalls—the watercourse equivalent to Pentecost's rushing, mighty wind—are sounding the souls of more and more of us. Jesus promised, "He that believes in Me, as the Scripture has said, out of his heart will flow rivers of living water" (John 7:37).

He was speaking of the Holy Spirit who is the sole "Channeler" of divine life and truth to this present world. To open to Him is to open to Christ's fullest and richest release. The promise is still the same: "In your seed shall all the nations of the earth be blessed." And the path for personal pursuit is still unchanged: redig the wells.

Centuries flow by and everything is changed. Millennia pass but nothing is different.

There are no theological mysteries, administrative secrets, ecclesiastical structures or marketing techniques waiting to be discovered as keys to tomorrow's triumphs. Isaac learned the principle long ago: however much you've been given, the time comes when you must press in for your own experience of God.

Nothing new is promised. Only something fresh. Even the taste of new wine hasn't changed since the beginning.

The passion for fullness is not a search for some sensuous spiritual sensation. It's a quest for God Himself—a return to the Fountain of our being that the fullness of His purpose for us in Christ be realized.

Without restriction.

Without inhibition.

CHAPTER

5

"What I don't quite understand," said Jill, "is how we didn't see the lettering?" "Why, you chump!" said Scrubb. "We did see it. We got into the lettering. Don't you see? We got into the letter E in ME ...." From *The Silver Chair*, by C.S. Lewis

Within These Walls

What could possibly inhibit anyone's full-hearted passion for fullness?

The genuineness of my concern for the world and its need, or of my desire for God's fullest and best is at stake. If the subject of "spiritual passion" finds me slow or hesitant—too cautious in response, I need to find out "Why?" Of course, there are real and practical reasons why many feel a caution toward a free and open availability to a raw outpouring of the Holy Spirit. Thoughtful, seeking hearts often deal with persistent questions: What will a full surrender to a passion for God's fullness in the life of His Spirit do to me?

- Will it open me to divisiveness and sectarian bigotry; "pulling me over the edge" into the vain supposition that I am now a member of the avant-garde—a spiritually elite group?

- Will it produce a passivity toward purity of life, preoccupying me with "experiences," giving place to feelings to the point of sacrificing my priority of godly conduct and moral integrity?

- Will it launch me on such a quest for wonders and revelations from God that I begin deviating from or twisting the timeless truth of His consummate, conclusive revelation in the eternal scriptures of the Bible—neglecting the counsel of His Holy Word?

We're wise if we ask these questions, for the history of the church—past and present—is littered with cases of passion gone awry. Every Christian knows at least one horror story, either through associations or hearsay. How often have sincere but naive believers been seduced by a cult or some aberration of Christian tradition? The disastrous result was the bitter fruit of passion which became misguided as they pursued an unqualified "quest for God."

However, bad endings are avoidable when right beginnings are made. The questions we've raised can and should be resolved, but they should not be allowed to quench or temper our passion. Facing them squarely, we can arrive at balanced answers, and then feel free to release ourselves to the Holy Spirit's call—to sensibly *and* passionately pursue *all* God has for each of us today in the life and power of His Holy Spirit.

The first question addresses the problem of divisiveness. This "bugaboo" seems to plague us whenever the subject of "Spirit-fullness" comes up. I had to face it myself, at a crucial time in my own life several years ago. Solutions didn't come without sensitive persistence, but some practical lessons were learned. I found a way to dissolve the fear and the power of divisiveness. It came about when two congregations—one Baptist and one Pentecostal—came to the edge of divisive strife between them.

A LOCAL TEMPEST
I groaned as I hung up the phone, "Oh, no! I can't believe this!"

Signalling my secretary, I asked her to find the phone number of Harold Fickett, pastor of the Van Nuys First Baptist Church, where under his gifted leadership and great expository preaching, that congregation became one of America's largest churches.

Carefully reviewing the facts that had just been given to me via the call I'd received, I shuddered inwardly, thinking, "I hate it— literally *hate* sectarianism like this!" My irritation was levelled not at Harold, whom I was seeking to get on the line, but at what had been said from the pulpit of my own church the preceding Wednesday night.

I had been out of town ministering elsewhere, and a pulpit guest—sincerely motivated I suppose, but foolishly blinded by the small-minded competitiveness so often infecting the body of Christ—had given a report which had sent out shockwaves now threatening the fellowship between two congregations.

I hadn't heard what had happened until Monday morning, when I received a call saying that the day before Dr. Fickett had made public mention of what had been said at our church the preceding Wednesday. He declared it untrue, asserting that he had placed a personal telephone call to the principals involved, inquiring and setting the record straight.

Had I been he, I would have made the same call.

The setting for this local tempest was 1972, when the Billy Graham organization was preparing for its great crusade in Korea. Somehow, somewhere, my pulpit guest had received information which led him to believe what he triumphantly declared to our midweek assembly. Apparently seeking to illustrate the ever-broadening acceptance of charismatic phenomena, he had said:

"I have just heard that in training of counselors for altar work at his forthcoming Korean crusade, Billy Graham's team is instructing every one of the trainees to be baptized in the Holy Spirit, and encouraging them to speak in tongues!"

Not having been present, I had first—before calling Dr. Fickett—asked one of our pastoral team what the congregation's response had been.

"Rather mixed," he answered.

"Some were almost ecstatic—a few visitors I suppose. But most of our people responded as you would think—and hope. They seemed dubious for the most part, looking at one another as if to say, 'Hard to believe; but if it's true, what does it *really* prove?'"

Curiously enough, one of the First Baptist Church's congregation had been visiting that evening—a staff member, who was understandably upset and who gave this report to his pastor the next day. That's why Harold called the Graham offices, verified his suspicions of the report's fallacy and told his congregation as much.

I was disturbed in *two* ways—not only over the guest speaker's remark, but also because Harold's reference to our church, in issuing the appropriate correction, presented a face unrepresentative of our true spirit. I certainly didn't blame him for confronting an issue which understandably upset him, but I did regret the fact that this held great potential for damaging interchurch agreement. He knew I was not present at the meeting, but he didn't know how I would have responded had I been. Now, I was deeply concerned about how reckless words spoken at our church could horribly misrepresent my spirit as a pastor and our heart as a congregation.

Dr. Fickett came on the line, greeting me in his typically grand style—a giant of a leader with a disarming forthrightness and genuine love for people: "Hello, Jack. How are you today!"

"Hello, Harold," I began cautiously. "Not very well, I'm afraid."

"Well, what's the matter?"

"Harold, I want to ask you to be patient with me for a minute or two, because I need to set something on the table that concerns me as much as it does you. But first, I want to ask your understanding and forgiveness."

"Go ahead, Jack," he invited.

"I'm calling because of what was said by the speaker at our church last Wednesday. I'm sorry about that and, not being here, I was unable to do anything about it at the time. I know you heard about it, and I also know that you investigated the matter, and have made an appropriate refutation of the purported facts.

"But besides that, what I am essentially calling for is to tell you two things you don't know—because I believe it's important to our relationship and to the Body of Christ here in the Valley."

TESTING A RELATIONSHIP

We had actually been together only once, nearly two years before, shortly after I had come to this small San Fernando Valley pastorate which was now growing rapidly. He had accepted my suggestion that we become acquainted over lunch. Warmly welcoming the idea, he hosted our meal, and thus—though it was not deeply established—we had a relationship of sorts. Because our churches were only two blocks apart, our relationship was especially important, and now I felt it was being tested.

"The first thing I want you to know, and which you couldn't know without my telling you," I continued, "is that I'm grateful you investigated and discovered the inaccuracy of what was said. The truth didn't surprise me at all. I didn't believe it when I heard it myself."

He was quiet. I could tell he was somewhat puzzled.

"The second thing you don't know is this, Harold." I paused, feeling peculiarly pained deep within myself. "Brother," I said gently, "even if I had heard that and discovered it to be true, I wouldn't have made a public issue of it."

"You wouldn't?" He sounded amazed. "Why, I would have thought you would have considered it a *victory!*"

"Well, I wouldn't have. That may surprise you, but it's true."

"Jack," this princely leader responded, "you're right. I'm *very* surprised to hear what you're saying. It certainly reveals that we have need for a great deal more fellowship, doesn't it?"

Of course, I agreed, and before long we did experience a furthering of our relationship, and I am delighted to be able to claim Harold Fickett as a friend. He's in retirement now, yet still stands as a model of pulpit greatness. And it means a lot to know he calls me "friend" also.[1]

FOUR FACTORS LEARNED

The Valley-wide teapot-tempest was stilled that day, but the winds of adversity which blow from the lips of many of us in the Church at large badly need to be quelled. And I relate this anecdote because I believe it contains a combination of factors which breed division and beget resistance to the Holy Spirit's present efforts at drawing us together. What took place between two churches not only shows the potential for confusion, division and strife, it also reveals the possibilities for understanding and mutual fellowship. Reviewing it, consider some lessons we might learn:

First, the *setting* involved an apparent "upstart": a new, smaller group, seeming to have hatched like a chick, and now irritatingly beginning to peck at the heels of its splendid rooster-parent. It happens all the time.

Renewal groups so quickly rise and can be so quick to "peck" at those groups who have been around longer—who have "paid the price" for the church's presence in the community. Too often, too little if any respect for or deference toward the original group is shown. The "new" so easily forget that their existence depended on forebears.

There is *nothing* of renewal, revival or divine blessing being manifest in charismatically disposed groups, but that the fountain-head originally flowed from solidly established, historic church groups who have stood the test of time. It is understandable that the older group is tempted to impatience if not anger when their offspring, whether literally or figuratively, jauntily claim superiority.

Our church was the newcomer. The words of the guest seemed smug, as though arrogantly claiming to test the tradition represented by the neighboring church. In contrast, our commitment to respect the historic group's integrity of purpose, however different our ways, brought a peace where conflict could have wedged God's people apart.

Second, the *situation* involved a presumed mistake, but was based on a frequently practiced ploy. How frequently are we who doctrinally differ tempted to exploit and expound our distinctives as though they elevated us to a platform of superior worth! The pulpit guest at our church, as wrong as he was both in his facts and in his use of supposed information, clearly gave the impression that "our side is winning." The "us and them" mentality which infests the body of Christ has created an environment in which the spirit of competition, if not hostility, reigns. While our future fellowship developed the kind of relationship which would keep such an episode from recurring, it isn't surprising that Dr. Fickett didn't bother to call me first. When any of us erect walls to mark our battle lines on critical subjects, those walls cast shadows which leave both sides in the dark.

RELATIONSHIP WITHOUT UNIFORMITY

Third, the *story* reflects the possibilities of relationship without uniformity; of mutual appreciation and benefit without resigning our distinctives or refusing to listen to one another. Both the pastors involved avoided the stereotypical mold their backgrounds might have dictated.

My ability to approach Dr. Fickett when the situation required it was based on his early acceptance of me. Though a renowned pastor to thousands, widely published and broadcast, he took time to fellowship with a younger pastor of a small, neighboring congregation. His absence of self-importance, with his will to reach across lines of clear difference, allowed my boldness to telephone when the problem arose.

Further, I know my nonthreatening, unaccusing approach helped that day I called. Still, his readiness to accept an explanation *and* to admit the need for more open fellowship manifests qualities from which we may all learn. Our exchange—and ongoing friendship—changed neither of our doctrinal postures. However, it is unquestionable that we both hold a respect for the grace of God manifest through our distinctive emphases. I know this is true, for I've said as much with sincerity, and so has he.

But *most of all,* and at the heart of my reason for relating this event, is this final point:

Fourth, this episode reveals the seldom perceived fact that "speaking in tongues," or "*being right* about the sign of Spirit-fullness" for most Pentecostals or charismatics *isn't*—or certainly never should be—an issue worth separating fellowship from other Christians. As I told Dr. Fickett, even if the purported statement had been true it would not have made sufficient difference to me that I would parade it. This amazed him because of a perspective so many of us have on those who differ from us. We tend to presume their "distinctive" is the *whole* of their emphasis rather than simply an integrated part of their Christian faith—most of which is common to us all. It is unfair to one another to forget that *before* and *beyond* our differences, there is a broad body of common ground we each treasure:

- We all worship the One True and Living God.
- We all seek to glorify Jesus Christ His Son.
- We all claim redemption through the Blood of His Cross.
- We all are indwelt by His precious Holy Spirit.
- We all attest to the absolute authority of the Bible.
- We all sing. We all pray. We all serve. We all love.

That is, "we all love" until fear crowds out the love, or antagonism removes space for its presence. But fear and any possibility of antagonistic posturing can easily be evicted if the light of love's simplest glimmerings is allowed between us. Once I choose to *hear* the heart of my perceived adversary, I may discover he is no enemy at all—only a partner in humanity who fears misunderstanding or rejection. Consider the two pastors in this case study.

Pastor Fickett didn't want to be perceived as inattentive to a report he doubtless knew was fallacious even before he confirmed it being so. Pastor Hayford's heart was softened toward his neighbor-pastor in recognizing his action was that of any good shepherd: seeking to shield his sheep, not simply to swat at a neighbor.

Pastor Hayford didn't want to be perceived as a small-minded bigot, championing a small issue as though it were the watershed point of Christian history. Pastor Fickett heard his heart and was receptive, recognizing his Pentecostal neighbor had higher priorities than he realized—that we were brothers needing to know each other better.

LABYRINTHINE WALLS

The entire encounter symbolizes so much.

As I remembered it, an abstract vision took shape, a scene of us who live within the larger family of God, so mixed, yet so diverse. It was a picture of walls arranged in a labyrinthine manner, where each person within the walls perceived himself to be in a separate compartment, only to later discover they were all together in the same mammoth maze. Then the mental image cleared. I suddenly realized I had read this in a children's story years before.

The Silver Chair, one of C.S. Lewis' seven-volume *Chronicles of Narnia*, involves a search for the lost Prince Rilian. Aslan, a lion, and the dominant character common to all the Chronicles (a characterization of Christ, the Lion of Judah), has given the children a series of signs which, when followed, will lead them to the Prince.

Traveling with these guidelines, the children fumble along to the point where they are now seeking the next sign: "You will find a writing on a stone . . . It will tell you what to do." Because they are engulfed in a snowstorm at the time they reach the outskirts of the ruined city where they are to find the stone-writing, they do not even realize they are there.[2]

Shortly, they stumble into a trench, and for some time wander in and out among the stone walls through which the trenches weave in an apparently meaningless fashion. It is only much later, when their search has been suspended through their being captured, held by a band of giants, that they make a discovery. From the elevation of their captors' dwelling high on a hill, they look down upon the trenches which had bewildered them. Only then can they see that the stone walls of the trenches were the very words for which they were searching; a giant labyrinthine maze of raised, engraved letters—the key to their finding the Prince.

And how often it is so with us.

Together we are searching for our King, the Prince of Peace— seeking His presence and power for the fulfillment of His Kingdom purposes.

He has written in words more permanent than stone, "Love one another . . . ." He has prayed we would *be one* "that the world may know." Yet we find ourselves separated by "the words," each of us groping forward with hearts desiring to please our Prince.

What snowstorm has blurred our vision that we do not recognize our situation? What giants will it take to capture us until we look with longing on the key to our quest?

Can we neutralize the restrictive power of these walls of perceived separation (which often become walls of outright adversity!)? The answer is "Yes!" If we will rise above our limiting viewpoints we will discover that we are *not* in separate circles, but simply "feeling our way" through the eternal Word of God, missing the larger *key* word—Love—by reason of our preoccupation with its parts! Can we see it *now*?

We are together "in the trenches" and are all between the same walls—already one people in one place! Though we each "know in part and prophesy in part," and presently see one another "through a glass darkly," our Savior's call to let love prevail can bring us to "one accord."

FISSION AND FUSION

In the atomic structure of spiritual things, we know from divine revelation that when one people in one place come unto one accord, the critical mass has come to the place of either fission or fusion. We need both: *fission* to split human walls of resistance or fear and *fusion* to melt us all together unto a massive release of divine power in the world!

- What do we each have to contribute to this holy release of power?
- What are the resources we are wise to perceive in one another?
- How might we learn that *all* our distinctives are but a "knowing in part"?
- Can we learn to appreciate that "part" another holds dear but we may not!?

- When will we see we are each tributaries designed to flow together to a surging Amazon of Holy Spirit workings in the church?

The passion for fullness is a passion fired by *love*—love for Christ, love for God's Word, and a loving *will* to learn greater love for all the members of the vast family of our Father. Jesus Himself established the criteria for our mutual acceptance: "He who is not against us is on our side . . . . He who is not with Me is against Me, and he who does not gather with Me scatters abroad" (Mark 9:40; Matthew 12:30).

His words recommend simple interpretation, uncluttered by my own definitions which determine that "against Him" is anyone who is "against my way of viewing things." His is the church because He is its Savior. Ours is to learn to love one another, because we have been "so loved!"

We might be wise to back away a few paces so we can more clearly read the great word carved in the tables of Holy Scripture:

If you love Me, keep My commandments.
A New commandment I give to you:
Love one another as I have loved you.

All of us who love Christ and name Him as Savior and Lord are somewhere in the trenches among those letters. With a higher perspective we can see it: One people in one place, between walls which only seem to divide because we haven't caught the vision we need. When we see it and open our hearts to each other, the world will see it too.

As we begin to come out of the church's walled shadows, they'll begin to come out of the world's dark.

When they do, let's show them a rainbow.

CHAPTER

6

Immediately I was in the Spirit; and behold a throne set in heaven and One sat on the throne ... And there was a rainbow around the throne, in appearance like an emerald ... and there were seven lamps of fire burning before the throne, which are the seven Spirits of God. Revelation 4:2-4

The Rain and the Rainbow

There is a magnificence to the rainbow.

It's not only natural to associate such splendor with God's throne of power, it's scriptural. Both Ezekiel and John describe seeing a rainbow glory surrounding the presence of the Almighty One. Messages abound in that rainbow:

There is *beauty* where His fullness dwells.
There is *breadth* in the full color band of the spectrum.
There is *variety* revealed in the wonder of His works.

There is also another simple message: *Rainbows appear where refreshing mist or rain is present.* That's a not-so-subtle clue to my need to keep open to the spiritual "rain" which characterizes the Holy Spirit's *refreshings*—His outpouring of refilling and renewal to our souls.

Eight hundred years before the birth of Christ, the prophet Joel used this terminology in forecasting the church's birth. As the predictor of Pentecost, he declared:

> Rejoice in the Lord your God; for He has given you the former rain, and the latter rain in the first month . . . And it shall come to pass afterward that I will pour out My Spirit on all flesh . . . on my menservants and on my maidservants I will pour out My Spirit in those days. And I will show wonders in the heavens and in the earth . . . (See Joel 2:21–32).

On the church's birthday, the apostle Peter seized Joel's word picture and not only said what was happening was God's fulfillment of the prophecy, he pressed the truth right down to our day today—"For the promise is to you and to your children, and to all who are afar off, as many as the Lord our God will call" (Acts 2:39).

Today, we need the rain, and the rainbow glory with it.

Those rainbow qualities of beauty, breadth, variety and refreshing—clear traits of the Father's fullness—well might draw us to the Throne of God, to bow there in His presence and be enlarged and enlightened. Not only can we be enlarged in soul as we are filled with His Person in worship, but may we allow Him to enlighten us as to our limited personal perceptions of His "glory." That rainbow radiance is a revelation of the Almighty God's multifaceted splendor, not the cheap glimmer of a New Age crystal. An open-heartedness to His manifold wisdom reflected in His glory can help us see any tendencies toward smallness or narrow-mindedness in ourselves.

Pursuing God's fullness will inevitably challenge my private or sectarian viewpoints. It confronts whatever may confine my vision to only those facets of God's rainbow workings which appeal to my taste. Doctrinaire tunnel vision can breed my color blindness to the broad-brush workings of His grace in other Christian groups beyond the "color band" of my own circle or experience.

MY FAVORITE COLOR?

Think of the implications of this concept. How does the idea of God's "rainbow glory" require my humility before His vast variety of workings confront my becoming too selective as to "my favorite color"?

For example, Christian love obviously recommends we all live with that social sensitivity and adult maturity which disallows our disposition to that kind of "color preference" called "racial prejudice." But even if I would refuse to tolerate racism or cast an ethnic slur, how prone am I to accept my closedness toward a fellow believer holding a doctrinal stance different from mine? In the rainbow light of God's Throne, can I see how my doctrinaire attitude, my preoccupation with *my* "authentic orthodoxy" or prized emphases, may be a case of "color preference"? It's tough to admit it, but in settling for "my favorite color" while accusing another of tastelessness or immaturity for theirs, I may be as guilty of prejudice as any racial bigot. Though someone's doctrine or practice differs from mine, if they indeed love Christ and seek to glorify Him, I *must* come to terms with—and eliminate—my prejudice. It's more than a matter of social taste. It's a requirement of spiritual grace.

A few years ago I received an invitation to speak to a group of pastors in my area—leaders in a denomination with an extremely well-known distinctive. I had, in fact, studied their group while I was in college—my text being a handbook of "cults and Christian sects." The book was clear in its priorities, wanting to instill a sensitivity for biblical truth and to protect against the corrosive effect of error on the soul. And the author was faithful to distinguish between "damning error" and "questionable emphases." He carefully discerned how that all cults were essentially born of demonic confusion, while Christian sects were products of doctrinal questions on issues not generally held by the larger part of the Church. He did not blacklist the "sects," but he only noted their idiosyncrasies rather than declaring them completely erroneous.

Somehow I succumbed to something I suspect most other readers did. Those "sects with questionable emphases" became lumped in my mind with the "cults of damning error." Even though the issues distinguishing "sects" were not considered conclusively destructive, the whole flavor of the approach imprinted the reader with serious doubts. The suspicion was inescapable: that something of an order of leprosy lurked within each "sect"—ready to threaten anyone exposed to people of that group. Now, here I was about to address one of these "suspect" groups. I decided to accept the invitation.

I knew there was a risk. Someone might hear of my speaking to that group and initiate the rumor, "Jack Hayford is going 'weak' on sound doctrine." But I set the date anyway, deciding to accept the risk. I was more interested in listening to the wisdom in the maxim, "Some people spend so much time protecting their reputation that they lose their character." Fellowship with—and learning from—people who love Christ had to be more important than protecting myself from the possibility of "guilt by association." Three things amazed me as a result of the experience:

1.   The people seemed no different from *any* group of evangelicals I have ever met. They worshiped Christ, revered God's Word and showed a gentle graciousness that would warm anyone's heart.

2.   They were unusually gratified by my coming, and I learned why. It wasn't until I was with them that I could detect something of a residue of pain inflicted by the general rejection they have received from evangelicals like me. How frequently they must have been hurt when similar invitations such as they gave me had been shunned or scorned. They didn't say this, I simply sensed it; and my coming somehow affirmed them as "one of the Family." Had you met them as I did, I think you would agree such acceptance was something they deserved from those of us outside their sector of the church.

3.   Then, I learned that their doctrinal "peculiarity" wasn't as peculiar as I had been taught. As the days passed while I

was with them, the comfort of acquaintance and a growing familiarity with one another allowed me to venture an inquiry into their "emphasis." While I could not and did not agree (they didn't ask or expect me to), I did learn (a) they had better biblical reasons for their point than I had been taught they had, and (b) it was *not* an issue worth our avoiding one another's fellowship—*ever*.

What might we all learn if we take such "risks"?

To determine to be open to "all the fullness of God" *will* require a humbling of my preferences. It will *not* require that I *be* everything or *do* what everyone does, whatever beauty I may find in the ways of God in another group's midst. But it will require my learning to accept—humbly to admit my limits instead of fearfully or pridefully drawing my boundaries.

Is it possible for any of us to completely span the spectrum of God's "multifaceted wisdom"? What scholar presumes to "know all"? Who among us is pretentious enough to become so cocksure of our own righteousness that we despise the righteous work of God in those we neither know nor understand well? Should we not bow in reverence every time we encounter His power, His workings or His worship—even in settings and by styles with which we are unfamiliar? Should we not humbly exclaim again: "Oh, the depth of the riches both of the wisdom and knowledge of God! How unsearchable are His judgments and His ways past finding out! For who has known the mind of the Lord? Or who has become His counsellor?" (Romans 11:33, 34).

ANYTHING GOES-ISM
But questions press forward in our minds:

- "Doesn't this abandon us to the oblivion of 'anything goes-ism'?" "Are all criteria for evaluation to be submerged beneath an ooze of generosity—a so-called love—and thereby *any* belief, *any* practice or *any* proposition be sanctified as a hitherto undiscovered band of light on the heavenly spectrum?"

- "What about landmarks, plumb lines or standards to determine boundaries, measurements or expectations?"

And, of course, these concerns are valid. Indeed, how *much* will "all the fullness of God" tolerate? How far will the passion for fullness take us? Does the call to be *stretched* demand we be *snapped* like an overextended rubber band? It's a challenge to find a solid answer and a greater one to apply it. It requires my becoming as passionate about Christ's body as I am about God's Word, for *both* are involved in "all the fullness of God" which is in Christ.

I'm duped by misplaced priorities if I am able to separate those realities—His church and His Word. We need to find the meeting point where our similarities intersect and our differences are allowed. Is it possible the passion for fullness can bring us to the place that we can accept each other at points of *convergence* on biblical essentials? And that we could *still* love each other notwithstanding our points of *divergence*? The question is this: If the *essence* of living faith is present in a fellow-Christian's stance toward Christ and the Word, am I willing to humble myself in the face of those things wherein I differ with him? And even *further*, will I be willing to listen to the heart of those who see things in God's Word which elude me, or even which I may never accept?

ANSWERING HUMILITY'S CALL

That call to humility requires *more* than just toleration. It calls for a willingness to humbly investigate as well.

If I accept that I alone am not sufficient—none of us are—to comprehend the full scope of God's wisdom and workings, then I will recurringly face this decision: When I find (a) operations of God's Spirit or (b) truth claimed from His Word, *either* being new to me, will I answer humility's call? Will I be willing to ask myself: "Could there be something here I am to learn of greater 'fullness'?" When viewing someone who has experienced "times of refreshing from the Lord," but within a rainbow color I'm not as familiar with, I face a choice. Scorn and spurn or listen and learn.

I must learn to deal with my temptation to prefer the coziness of my own closed system, and the inclination to describe those experiencing the Holy Spirit's "rain" as merely being "all wet"!

THEN HOW WILL WE KNOW?

The "rainbow" reality of God's multifaceted wisdom confronts me and calls for my willingness to listen—to learn—to be open. But if we're to learn an openness to broader workings of God, it *is* necessary to ask, "How will we know soundness from folly?"

The call to fullness is not a call to gullibility. Rather than being either lovelessly rigid or naively undiscerning, can we decide on guidelines that will allow *all* of us more freely to respond to each other, and to that which stretches us?

There are two reasons it is desirable for us to establish a criteria for *soundness*, which neither pleads anyone's private position nor resists God's sovereign work: (1) it will broaden my *availability* to the Holy Spirit's present work, and (2) it will assure my *sensitivity* to the Bible's timeless truths. Further, having a gauge to guarantee I'm not "going overboard" can release me to a more confident availability to the Holy Spirit's work. I will become (1) more ready to welcome His *comforting* works, refreshing and renewing me, and (2) more receptive to His *confronting* works, which can shake me by His power and shape me with His purification.

What then might be a beginning guideline for knowing when "something new" is truly "God at work"? I propose the following:

- That the birthmark of God's authentic working will always be the same: *Jesus Christ* will be central in all *worship, walk* and *witness* according to God's *Word.*

Thus, the forms of *worship* may vary, but Christ will always be exalted; the emphases in the believer's *walk* may differ, but Christlikeness will always be pursued; the approaches to evangelistic *witness* will find variety in style, but souls will always be in the process of being brought to Christ the Lord; and, God's *Word* may be interpreted differently at points, but its authority will always be absolute.

Here is a basic Book-of-Acts standard for evaluating spiritual breakthrough.

This proposition is clearly not a detailed doctrinal grid over which we individuals or movements can be stretched in inquisition. But these basics provide a constant, acknowledging a fundamental fruitfulness which removes our being too quick to suspect or reject and thereby to become deaf to something "the Spirit is saying to the churches." The "color" of the fruit may differ, but its "goodness" will be verifiable. (1) Jesus will be exalted, (2) practical purity valued, (3) living worship present and (4) God's Word honored. These are simple Book of Acts criteria which declare fellowship without the addiction of sectarian bias:

First: Jesus Christ will be exalted with heartfelt worship. Their preaching and purity are not mere formalities, but expressed with praise and adoration. Details of structure, variations in liturgy or taste in music are not the issue: vital *Life* is (Acts 2:46–47; 8:8; 11:21–26).

Second: Pure hearts are submitted to Jesus Christ as Lord. Transformed living is the verifiable fruit of committed disciples. Various approaches to practical sanctification and special require-ments for proven holiness are not the issue. Rather, just as with the early church's first council decision, removal from immorality and idolatry is deemed enough to meet practical expectations (Acts 15:20; 19:12–20).

Third: Jesus Christ will be preached as Savior and the lost brought to Him. He is the primary focus, and His accomplished work as mankind's Redeemer the fundamental message. Doctrinal differences as to *how* this is viewed are not the issue at this point, simply that souls are being set free (Acts 2:36–38; 8:4–8; 16:30).

Fourth: They honor God's Word of truth. God's gift of His Word has one primary focus and fruit—to set free. It is not an instrument of intellectual enlightenment so much as a means of spiritual deliverance. Preaching style and interpretive refinements are not the issue; rather, the issue is that truth is liberating people from sin, death, bondage and hell—and that in this liberty they grow steadfastly by the Word of God.

This teaching is both sound and safe; it is based on and beckons us to live in the church's spirit of openness in Acts. Let us remember Gamaliel's judicious cautioning about taking too quick a stance against what we don't understand. And let us note the Jerusalem Council's breadth of receptiveness as it modeled a practice for our emulation (Acts 15:6–29).

Just as the explosion of the Holy Spirit's power in the first century created a dilemma for those steeped in their Judaism, similar explosions in the twentieth century have done the same with some of us steeped in our Christianity. Just as there was a ready disposition to reject Gentile believers who didn't meet the Jewish criteria for orthodoxy, so today are many of us trained in our various Christian sectors to do the same.

This habit of slicing up the body of Christ into "approved" and "disapproved" sections not only wounds deeply, it creates horrifying division. At times there is altogether too frequent a readiness to *amputate*—to declare someone whose experience differs from mine as "unsaved" or "questionable."

REJECTED BY A BROTHER

It was nearly thirty years ago, early in my ministry, that I was powerfully impacted by this problem. I learned a lesson through an incident which may make the retelling useful for you.

It was in Denver years ago as the first conference session of the National Association of Evangelicals convention had just concluded. I was hurrying toward a barely recognizable exit, taking a shortcut unnoticed by most of the throng, who were slowly crowding through more obviously located doorways.

I was only a few brisk strides from the exit when it opened ahead of me, and stepping through it—alone—was one of the most widely known spiritual leaders in the world. He was apparently slipping into the rear of the auditorium unobtrusively, to look over the site where later that day he would address this convention.

I was 28, a youthful minister whose life and thought in God's work was still being shaped by mentors, many of whom influenced me from a distance by their marked leadership. And here was one of them standing directly in front of me. It was a priceless moment for me, to have the opportunity personally to meet and greet someone I held in highest esteem, and whose life profoundly touched multitudes—including mine.

There being no one else nearby, it was easy to pause and introduce myself. Not wanting to presume upon his schedule, and being very careful not to appear cloying or maudlin in my manner, I quickly thanked him for his ministry as it had impacted mine. He smiled warmly, showing a genuine personal interest in me as I spoke, and then he asked, "Jack, where is your base of ministry?"

"Los Angeles," I answered. "I'm the National Youth Director for the Foursquare Church."

What happened in the next three seconds shattered me. With my response, his grip slackened and the hand he had gently placed on my shoulder slid to his side, as his expression changed. He didn't scowl, but the warm smile had been instantly replaced by a chilling stiffness. Excusing himself rather brusquely, he stepped by me and proceeded toward whatever destination was in mind before our brief encounter.

I almost reeled with the impact of the sudden transformation that my words had caused in him. One moment I had felt the strong affirmation of a respected leader, the next—immediately following the disclosure of my church affiliation—I was stunned by his quick and silently eloquent rejection. Continuing through the door toward which I had been hurrying, I slowed my pace dramatically. I virtually stumbled up the stairway to my room, my emotions ransacked and my mind whirling. Though I doubted he had intended to hurt me as he had, I was still plagued by the question: "Why am I so objectionable to this man whom I held in such esteem?" It would be ten years before I discovered the answer to that question.

It wasn't as though I begrudged the moment or bitterly carried it for a decade. I didn't. I had long since written it off as just one small incident that communicates unintended hurt among members of Christ's Body, when an unusual thing happened.

A REVERSE DISCOVERY

Wholly without any quest on my part, a minister friend told me of a most remarkable conversation. A personal acquaintance of his—a leading Pentecostal church executive—had met the leader who had stunned me by his actions ten years before. Two notable leaders of different doctrinal persuasions surprisingly found themselves seated beside each other on a commercial airline flight. What occurred was nothing short of amazing, for through their discussion that day, the Pentecostal was shocked to discover a startling fact. Until *that* day, and *that* conversation, the non-Pentecostal leader was perplexed by what he *thought* was Pentecostal doctrine. He believed that Pentecostals were convinced that no one had truly experienced salvation *unless they spoke in tongues*!

Needless to say, that time of interaction allowed the Pentecostal leader to correct his misconception and, in fact, the event precipitated a major step forward in interevangelical relations over the years to come. However, I was hearing this only days after it happened, and suddenly I made a reverse discovery of what had happened that day in Denver years before. That man hadn't rejected *me*. His cold departure was because he presumed I did not accept *him*! While nothing could have been further from the truth, the controlling power of the moment was not fact but perception.

I relate the incident because it seems to me to strike to the core of the dominant issue we must settle if Christ's *whole* church is ever to be free to advance unitedly with a passion for "all the fullness of God" abounding in our midst.

- We certainly can't if we don't have a mutual agreement on "who's saved"!
- None of us is likely to answer a call to "more of Christ and His power" if we feel we are viewed as less than "saved," less than "holy," less than "spiritual," or less than "worthy"

for simply being what we already are: Christians! People born again, alive in Christ, washed in the Blood of the Lamb and indwelt by the Holy Spirit of God!

- The love of Christ in the church can never be realized when those guilty of nothing more than tasting renewal, first-century life or the Holy Spirit's power, are branded— "deceived," "demon-possessed" or "seduced by Satan."

Is there a way to stop stepping on one another?

I think so, but it would require our accepting the central appeal of Paul's words to the Ephesians, words which define grounds for Christian agreement: "Till we all come to the unity of the faith, and the knowledge of the Son of God . . ." (Ephesians 4:13). Can we hear it? "The knowledge of the Son of God!" Here is the apostolic proposition: *Unity of the faith is never proposed in the Scripture on the basis of matching doctrinal emphases, but on the basis of our each knowing Jesus Himself.* He is the common ground upon which we can gather—the place where we can sing, "On Christ the Solid Rock we stand!"

Unlike classical human efforts seeking ecclesiastical union, these biblical grounds for spiritual openness, mutuality and fellowship focus on Christ Himself. Denominational structures and doctrinal differences or preferences become secondary as we answer one question: If we have all gathered around the same Jesus, are we not then partakers of the same salvation?

I think more of us agree than we realize.

We simply need to come together around the prism that casts the rainbow.

CHAPTER

7

prism (priz'm) n.: in optics, a transparent body,
as of glass, used for refracting or dispersing
light, as into the spectrum.

The Prism of Pleroma

Foremost in pursuing our passion for fullness, let this understanding predominate: *The passion for fullness is a passion for Christ
Himself!*

Jesus, the incomparable Son of God, is the One through
Whom the Father has manifest *all* His glory, fullness, purpose and
power.

"White" light is not the absence of color but actually the
convergence of *all* colors, and we've all seen what happens when
a beam of light is split, passing through a prism—whether in the
form of a raindrop, an angular piece of glass, a crystal jewel or
morning dew on a blade of grass—light separates into its
component colors, and there before us, in the splendor of the
spectrum, is the manifold brilliance of the rainbow.

So with our Lord Jesus Christ—the Light of the World. Sent
by the Father into our world in His pristine, white-light
perfection, He is the composite of the spectrum of God's Fullness.

Through Him every facet of the fullness of the Godhead has been unfolded to mankind.

- Ours is to receive the full revelation of all His work and wonders.
- Ours is to be enfolded by the glorious spectrum of His manifestations.

As Jesus Himself is the prism through Whom we have seen the glory of God, His full Person and works are the spread of divine color which is needed to brighten the world today.

ALLOWING "ALL" OF JESUS

Sitting with one of America's best known evangelists were a dozen pastors and church leaders representing several points on the spectrum of evangelicalism. I was there by reason of a growing relationship he and I had gained, even though his church tradition was considerably removed from my Pentecostal circles. We had come to know one another through a prayer relationship—and from that, a mutuality had developed which occasioned my being involved with this particular group in which he was confiding a concern.

He was anxious to cultivate young evangelists—people stirred with a zeal for winning the lost to Christ, and gifted to minister to large crowds as was the case with his ministry.

"If you were to tell me what your primary counsel would be in my influencing these young leaders, what would it be?" he asked.

Several at the large table expressed their thoughts, with a solid body of suggestions forthcoming. I enjoyed listening to them but it wasn't the only reason I remained silent. Because of the foremost concern I felt—and that was what the evangelist had asked for—I thought it best to hold my counsel unless specifically asked. And he did ask.

Even though several of those present had not spoken as yet, he turned to me and said, "Jack, I would be particularly interested in what you would say." I leaned forward in my chair, raising my arms to rest on the table and smiled: "I should have known you would be," and laughed as the other men chuckled with me. Calling him by his first name, I continued.

"You know, I was sitting here thinking, *I'm only going to speak if he asks me directly*, because I didn't want to seem to be advancing some sectarian agenda.

"But as all you fellows know, I don't carry my Pentecostal/charismatic experience on my sleeve, and I never have been contentious about my stance or witness in this regard. So when the question was raised as to what our *'primary counsel'* would be, I thought of the broad realms of human need that today's evangelist faces. I not only thought of the obvious need of eternal souls to hear the truth of the Gospel and receive Christ, and eternal life. I thought of the deep dimensions of bondage that so many have become enslaved by—drugs, liquor, sex, the occult, satanism. And I thought how the physical afflictions of mankind are no fewer than in Jesus' day, and how much His healing power is needed.

"I felt that to suggest you train young leaders in the arenas of healing and deliverance evangelism, along with basic, dynamic proclamation of the Word of the gospel, would sound as though I were peddling a sectarian bias. So I decided what I would say, and it's this: *However you train them, teach them to expect and allow Jesus to do everything He wants to do.*

"That doesn't create a human agenda of expectations, but simply puts the focus on Jesus Himself—in His changeless power and compassion for human lostness and need. If we don't school people to back away from *all* He is able to do, it will be enough to release Him to show His power however He wishes."

It wasn't hard to make this proposal. The evangelist himself, as well as the others present, knew my spirit in saying what I did. But further, they were agreeable to the fact that the focus was on Jesus—the Savior Himself, and not simply on "things God will do for you."

THE PASSION FOR "PLEROMA"

Just as the group at that table accepted the counsel I offered, even though the evangelist himself and nearly all there were *not* Pentecostal or charismatic, the focus on Christ Himself allowed them to set aside the resistance to the miraculous in which most of them had been schooled by their church background.

Oh, that we might all find a personal release—a fearlessness to welcome the full *pleroma* of the prism beam of Christ's Person to engulf us with all His splendor!

Pleroma (fullness) was Paul's favorite word for Christ.

He spoke to a culture which coddled mystical dreams about an idealistic oneness of unity in the universe, knitting all things into a full-orbed whole. Yet while the apostle stood diametrically opposed to these speculative notions, he offered an answer to the human hunger for a completeness which philosophic inventions could not satisfy.

The same is true today.

Our cities burgeon with longing souls seeking to "merge consciousness with the divine mind," while only meditating their way to abstraction and confusion. Earnest seekers probe exotic locations like Stonehenge and the Great Pyramid, hoping these mysterious sites may precipitate a "harmonic convergence" with the powers of the universe. The New Testament reveals how the early church answered the same heartcry; presenting the *pleroma*—the fullness of a Savior who was enough to enrich paupers in a spiritually bankrupt society. The church unleashed the fullness of Christ at all dimensions, *letting Him be God*—to save, fill, heal, strengthen, teach, lead, speak, deliver, reveal. The fullness of the Jesus who walked through Palestine was experienced walking in the person of those naming His Name and expecting His fullness to manifest itself through them. Human need was fully met by heaven's fullness fully available.

Evangelist James Robison put it adroitly. Citing the episode of the two apostles' encounter with the crippled man at the Beautiful Gate in Jerusalem, he touchingly described the need of the man—and the need of mankind. "And then," James shouted, "here came

Jesus all dressed up in Peter and John!" That's it! The hurt and lostness of our world long for people filled with Jesus. The cry is for more than doctrinaire religion—people long for freeing and fulfilling *contact!*

And that cry isn't offensive to God's ears.

He isn't irritated with the fumbling gropings of blinded souls seeking a *touch*, a sense of *warmth*, a surge of *power*, an embrace of *love*.

As surely as He sent His Son to *touch* the seeking soul with love and life, His plan today is to continue with the same offer of vital contact. Jesus still wants to *touch* people—through the hands of His body, His church—"the fullness of Him who fills all in all!"

That "touch" must be more than a philosophical trade-off, offering a new set of proper theological words for the world's barren philosophical ideas. Let the Word we preach and the words we speak be "with power"; let this be communicated with a presence of the Holy Spirit which transcends formulas and slogans. Let us also be certain our "touch" softens the soul and awakens the conscience unto repentance as Jesus' own tender power speaks through us. Just as surely as there was a darkness in Egypt that could be "felt," there is a light in the Holy Spirit's presence that is intended to be felt too. "The entrance of Your Word brings light," writes the Psalmist. This light is to attend our declaration of God's Word, and is full orbed in its scope—light that burns out sin, reveals Christ, enlightens the mind, warms the emotions, heals the body and fills the soul. A world wanting "contact" is not without a truth-filled answer to its search wherever Christ's fullness flows from such a touch.

THE APOSTOLIC KEY

This fullness, filling the church as it fills each member, is the *pleroma* which was the apostolic key to the early church's life. The "body" of believers knew "fullness" as more than metaphorical speech. By the Spirit's power, they were being filled with Christ's presence and purpose.

- He was the secret to their growth, ministry and maturity—the head and heart of the body He was expanding, reaching through and perfecting.

Growth: "Till we all come to the unity of the faith and the knowledge of the Son of God, to a perfect man, to the measure of the stature of the *Fullness* (*pleroma*) of Christ" (Ephesians 4:13).

Ministry: "But I know that when I come to you, I shall come in the *Fullness* (*pleroma*) of the blessing of the gospel of Christ" (Romans 15:29).

Maturity: "(that you may) know the love of Christ which passes knowledge; that you may be filled with all the *Fullness* (*pleroma*) of God" (Ephesians 3:19).

Further, *pleroma* not only summarized the source of effectiveness in the "body-life" of the church, it described the glorious dimensions of the Person of the church's *Lord*. His leadership was more than a theological concept. His presence actuated their life and witness as He filled their ministry with His.

- He was the Fountainhead of all grace, power and victory; the Giver of gifts, the King whose kingdom was coming through them and the Victor whose preeminence ensured their ongoing triumph.

Grace: "And of His *Fullness* (*pleroma*) we have all received, and grace for grace. For the law was given through Moses, but grace and truth came through Jesus Christ" (John 1:16, 17).

Power: "For in Him dwells all the *Fullness* (*pleroma*) of the Godhead bodily and you are complete in Him, who is the head of all principality and power" (Colossians 2:9, 10).

Victory: "And He is the head of the body, the church, who is the beginning, the firstborn from the dead, that in all things He may have the preeminence. For it pleased the Father that in Him all the *Fullness* (*pleroma*) should dwell" (Colossians 1:18, 19).

Concerning *pleroma*, one anonymous English writer stressed the divine intent that the concept was to extend beyond mere doctrine and to become pragmatically dynamic. *Fullness* is not merely to *excite* our minds but *ignite* our ministry. After developing the texts above, he wrote:

"But *pleroma* . . . has yet another side (than the theological). It is not only a gift, it is a task . . . Besides the indicative we have here an imperative: besides Christology, we have pneumatology.

"Paul prays that members of the community may be filled with the whole *pleroma* of God, and that they may grow up in the fullness of Christ.

"Through baptism and faith the Church has Christ's victory reckoned to it . . . Now this potent truth must also be actualized in our lives . . . ."

The six references and the truth they speak distill the essence of New Testament life and thought: that (1) just as *All* of the Godhead has been focused in Christ, (2) so *All* of Christ has now been focused in His church.

We are dealing with a continuum:

* The redemptive plan which God the Father began by incarnating His fullness in the Person of His Son . . .
* He has willed to be advanced throughout the earth by pouring that same fullness into the body of the church.

Thus, as with Jesus Himself, the church—each one of us!—is called and potentially equipped to deliver the fullness of the Father's life and love to anyone—to *everyone*! And as with Jesus' ministry, this mission is not only in *declaring* the Word, but in *demonstrating* It.

Incarnating its truth, each of us, in our lives,
speaking its life, each of us, with our tongues,
extending its love, each of us, with our arms,
touching mankind, each of us, in Jesus' Name and
with His power.

At each point on the spectrum of revelation, at every juncture
that God's Word relates to life, the focus on *fullness* is to call us to
completeness in our living and our witness. The world awaits a
Body which both *completely knows* and *completely shows* Jesus'
wholeness in the face of human brokenness.

THE FOCUS OF FULLNESS

The passion for fullness is a passion fired by *love*.

There is no question Jesus' prayer for unity is for greater reasons than mere "togetherness." He prayed, "That they may be one,
Father, even as we are one." He knew the flow of His power would
only be diminished by any fragmentation of His Body. His focus
on His Body's unity was not political but practical—that *all* the
world with *all* its need have *all* He has to give through *all* His
people! That's why we are wise to pursue so complete a passion for
Him that it melts any obstacles between us and any who love Him
too.

The passion for fullness does not destroy discernment.

It *does* abolish discrimination, and it does bring a loving willingness to learn greater love for all the members of our Father's
vast family. Jesus established the criteria for our mutual acceptance: "He who is not with Me is against Me, and he who does
not gather with Me scatters abroad" (Matthew 12:30).

His words recommend simple interpretation, uncluttered by
definitions which determine that "against Him" is anyone who is
"against my way of viewing things." His is the church because He
is its Savior: ours is to love one another, because He has "so loved"
us all!

In 1974 I was at a gathering of area pastors for a presentation
by Campus Crusade for Christ, as they set forth their "Here's Life"

campaign possibilities for our region. There seemed to be a una-
nimity in expectation and willingness to partner together in
evangelism until one church dissented.

"We find it difficult to consider participation," the spokesper-
son said. "Since such an outreach as this does not guarantee *which*
local congregation a convert might attend, we cannot conscien-
tiously join with you; seeing as, for example, someone may choose
to attend . . ." And with that, he nodded toward one of the pastors
present and named that man's congregation—specifically disap-
proving of the worthiness in their eyes that a new believer attend
such a place.

Everyone in the room felt the sting of the remark. It was such
a pitiful perspective and such a heartless demonstration of the
lengths to which our perfectionistic demands on one another may
cause us to overlook the foundations of our unity.

But there is a passion—a pursuit of the Spirit which can overcome any such discrimination due to differences. It will occur
when we recognize that *love for Jesus* is all He requires to denote
those who are "for Me." As long as I might take Him to mean,
"Anyone against *me* (Jack) is against Jesus," I shall always find
grounds to separate from others—and deem myself holier for having done so. But when we instead honestly acknowledge what the
Savior *does* mean, we can open to more of *Him*—both in the
diversity of His people and the distinctives of their viewpoints on
His manifold fullness.

GROUNDS FOR OPENNESS

Our discerning of foundational priorities—the ultimate
grounds of living faith—is not surrendered in showing such openness. We are not guilty of appealing to a watery syncretism.
Syncretism is that practice of reducing living faith to pointless
platitudes, finding the lowest common denominator of beliefs
sought in order to effect a secularized unity. The bottom line is
usually something on the order of belief in birds, bees and
flowers—hardly equivalent to the Word, the Lord and the Blood.
Instead, our quest is grounded in a *love* for Christ and an *honor*

due His Saviorhood—the *highest* common ground we can ever find. In accepting our mutual focus on Him as the grounds of our unity, we are not throwing discretion to the winds, only sectarianism. We will thus lovingly greet one another, beyond our differences; we will be able to meet one another on the ground of the ultimate certainty. I think it's safe to name that "ground."

It's called Calvary.

Our groundedness in the Cross of Christ is the solid foundation for all faith, the sound footings for building unity, the joint understanding producing fellowship, and the central point from which all authority for our ministry is granted.

We're passionate about that.

Our passion for fullness, as a current quest for all Christ's power and its dynamic breakthrough in our world, is anchored in the Cross.

The Tree of Life raised in the New Testament to offer salvation to mankind is more than a Roman stake driven into the soil "on a hill far away." *Christ's Cross is the fountain of fullness, from which any passion for "more of Him" must begin.*

- Here is the place we find His love for us.
- Here is where we ought to be able to affirm the same for one another.

Whatever varied points we may represent on the spectrum of God's workings in the church, here—at the Cross—is the place His completed work of salvation does more than *provide* grounds for mutual acknowledgment—it demands it. He has bought each of us with His blood-price. He has birthed us into one family. He has made us blood brothers and sisters—in *Him*, by His Cross.

ROOTED IN CONVICTIONS

Certain convictions root our relationship together, because these truths are settled in the soil of Calvary-ground, to which we have all come and been forgiven.

These grounds are not lightly taken. We hold no glib notions about the fact that foundational essentials must be affirmed if *true* fullness is to fill all our lives and thereby all the church.

To release us from separatism, to cease rejection, to open to *breadth* without the fear of violating *basics*, to give place to passion for "*more*" without seeming to minimize the *grandest*, let us come together to Calvary. Here, on these grounds, let us magnify the *fullness of salvation* as it has been broken open to us through Jesus' Cross. A focus on this foundational point of fullness can break the deadlock of fear that binds Christians apart rather than together.

- How many sincerely *fear* violating the fundamental grounds of our faith in Christ? It's an appropriate "fear," as that word is defined by its classic usage which actually means *reverence*.
- How many wonder if a passion for the *manifest power* of the Spirit in their lives might lead to an indifference toward or a diminishing of their passion for the *magnificent power* of the Cross *above all?*

Let such fears and questions cease as we come to the point where the prism of the *pleroma* broke open the splendor of the spectrum of God's power. On these affirmations of our *need* and His *supply* of *full* salvation, we can stand united—*knowing we know and agreeing that we agree.* Consider this fourfold statement as such a starting place.

FOUR AFFIRMATIONS

1. *Let us affirm the lostness and sinfulness of man.*

Let us uniformly affirm our belief that *nothing* of our own goodness contributes to our salvation, and that *nothing* but Christ's accomplishment on the Cross can save us. Fullness of salvation is what we believe has been provided in Christ because fullness of salvation is what mankind needs.

Let us affirm these grounds for full salvation: (1) Jesus gave His atoning life-blood to pay the ransom price for our forgiveness and release; (2) Jesus died as a substitute to pay the death penalty for our sin; and (3) Jesus rose again from the dead to verify His victory in our behalf over sin, death and hell. We concur that "if

One died for all, then all died" (2 Corinthians 5:15). The lostness of mankind—individually and as a race—is not an optional opinion with us. The "saved" know they need salvation.

2. Let us affirm the uniqueness and finality of Jesus Christ.

As to Christ's uniqueness, we say that only a sinless Savior could pay the death-wages of sin and rise again. If He had been at all tainted by human sin either by birth or by one incident of failure, there would have been no salvation. But His virgin birth establishes His uniqueness and freedom from genetic taint, being begotten by the Father. And the Father's testimony attests to His complete sinlessness: "This is my beloved Son in whom I am well pleased."

As to Christ's finality, we affirm that there are no alternative programs for human redemption. "Neither is there salvation in any other, for there is no other name under heaven given among men whereby you must be saved" (Acts 4:12). While none of us are sufficient to answer the questions evoked by the prospect of the eternal judgment of those outside Christ, we declare the merciful justice of God and affirm our confidence that in Christ both mercy and judgment have met and kissed each other. We leave the disposition of the lost to the hands of a just and merciful God, while affirming Christ's own words—that He *alone* is "The way, the truth and the life," and that "No man comes to the Father but by Me." As there are no alternative programs of human redemption, there are no alternative pathways to it.

3. Let us affirm the reality and victory of the Resurrection.

Fullness of salvation includes eternal life, to which we boldly confess our faith because of a Savior who literally, physically, has risen from the dead. We unite on these facts: His Resurrection proves His sinlessness, His dominion, and His truthfulness—His *sinlessness* because He verified His suffering to pay the death penalty for us; His *dominion* because He has mastered the power of death and hell; and His *truthfulness*, because He prophesied He would rise again on the third day, and He did. Thereby He has fully evidenced His ability to fulfill His promise to us that we *too* shall be resurrected from the dead.

4. *Let us affirm the availability of full forgiveness and justification.*
Faith in Jesus Christ acknowledges and receives the rescinded
record of sins which had accumulated against us (Colossians 2:14);
a release from condemnation nagging the conscience (Hebrews
9:13, 14); and the establishing of a wholly right relationship with
God, the Holy Judge of the universe and now, in Christ Jesus, one
Justifier who declares us "Not guilty! Now or ever!" (Romans 5:1).
That "justification" completely reconciles us to God, satisfies His
justice, and in acquitting us from sin, attributes the perfect record
of Christ's sinless holiness to each of us in the eyes of God
(Romans 4:5-8).

In the light of these four stated convictions, may we affirm and
declare:

- Personal faith in Christ a necessity, received through
  repentance and acceptance of grace unto new birth
  (John 1:12; 3:3-5); and,
- Receiving of the Holy Spirit, obedience to baptism and
  commitment to discipleship incumbent upon us
  (Acts 2:37-47).

These are not merely doctrinal notions, they are foundational
realities at the heart of living faith, vital hope and genuine love.

Various detailed elaborations, interpretations and applications
concerning these vital points exist among scores of different
Christian traditions. But is it possible that these essentials, so
foundational to our faith, may also provide grounds for mutual
acceptance and our prospective unity?

These four propositions make clear that our passion for fullness streams from the Cross and the finished work of Christ.
Further, they attest that our passion is not an ungrounded giddiness
that seeks new heights because it has never found real depth.

And more.

Agreement at Calvary can lead us to cease rejecting each other and start receiving the blessing and benefit of the "rainbow" of God's wisdom displayed in different ways among us.

BUT WAIT...

"But wait," a sincere voice pleads, "isn't there more to the basis of our faith than 'just Jesus and the Cross'?"

Such a question should not be shouted down as though demeaning the grandeur of Christ's work on Calvary. Don't presume the inquirer to be a cold-hearted legalist.

As the prism of the *pleroma* opens the fullness of the *Person* of Christ to us as *central* and the fullness of His *salvation* as *foundational*, so a *fullness of the Scriptures* is *essential* to us.

What about the Bible?

What will be our stance toward our source of certainty—the grounds of our *revelation* of "the truth as it is in Jesus"?

CHAPTER

8

Just as the fountain of salvation flows from Christ's Cross, the fountainhead of revelation is found in God's Word. They cannot be separated—the Word Incarnate in Christ and the Word inscribed in the Bible.

The Fullness of His Word

The man is unquestionably gifted. I would call him a contemporary prophet-teacher, though his system of interpretation would require him to deny that such an office even exists in today's church. His expository skills are virtually unsurpassed, and my respect for those skills have only deepened through my personal acquaintance with him.

Although we live and serve in different areas, occasional meetings over the years have allowed a somewhat formal friendship. One day, at a breakfast, I came to understand the passion in his *heart* for God's Word and was indelibly impacted by the integrity of his feelings. We were sharing general concerns related to our respective ministries, when at one point he turned to me, looking squarely into my eyes. Though his entire demeanor was well-controlled, his voice nearly broke with emotion as he spoke.

"Jack, I have this deep, deep desire to get *inside* the Word of God . . . To help people know *exactly* what it means. I can't escape it. It's what I believe my life is actually all about."

To hear his voice, to see his face, and *then*, to know the phenomenal effectiveness of his teaching ministry was to be able to
understand *both*—the man's mission as well as why he was so
effective at *trans*mission. He *does* do what he passionately longs to
do: he helps people *know* the Word and to long to know it even
more. It was a memorable moment to hear his words and sense the
passion of his heart in them.

To my view, that man is a model of the passion for fullness as
it bears on yearning to know the Word of God—the Holy
Scriptures. Yet, there is a certain dilemma faced today whenever
pressing for the experiential aspects of God's Spirit—a kind of
dichotomy seems present with some. Just as some Christians
conceive of a passionate pursuit of fullness in the Holy Spirit and
His gifts as neglecting something of Christ and His Cross, so
others fear such an emphasis will bypass the priority of biblical-
centeredness. It's an appropriate challenge that deserves a sound
answer.

THE FOUNTAINHEAD OF REVELATION

Let us begin by asserting that just as the fountain of salvation
flows from Christ's Cross, the fountainhead of revelation is found
in God's Word. These are our sources of *all* power: the source of
authority in life (the Cross) and of authority in witness (the
Word). Here is the *action* of the Redeemer (His works) and the
absolutes of the Revealer (His Word). They cannot be separated—
for they are *both* the Eternal Word—the Word Incarnate in Christ
and the Word inscribed in the Bible. Together they balance the
fullness of God's consummate and conclusive unfolding of Life
and Truth to mankind.

The passion for fullness must be "full of the Word" too, with a
posture as solidly stanced in the Scriptures as in the Cross. But
here we approach a question:

Are we passionate for the Word equally in its truth *and* in its
power? The passion for fullness calls me *into* the Word of God and
unto its implications. How many of us are tempted by the sweet

satisfaction of studying the Bible to stop with Its *examination* alone, when the Holy Spirit of Truth within It calls us to *incarnation*—to experience the *Life*-power in the Letter!

How vulnerable *any* of us may be to separate the truth of the Word from its present power reminds me of a second conversation with the same respected friend who displayed such passion for the Word of God. Our second conversation was curious in this respect, that what he said this time seemed to stand in peculiar contrast to our earlier talk.

It was years later at another of our rare opportunities for fellowship. On this occasion he confided to me a recent turmoil of soul he had experienced as the result of a family member's being diagnosed with a life-threatening condition. He related how, in the midst of the struggle, he felt moved to enter an extended fast, as he prayerfully sought God for the life of the loved one. He was, of course, aware that I knew his approach to the Bible is quite insistent that healings and miracles are not to be expected today.

As he spoke, his eyes searched mine, apparently looking to see if I would register surprise at his action. I didn't. Though I recognized that this was not normal behavior for him, I was careful not to register anything other than a warm acceptance of whatever he chose to share with me. I was touched by his faith-with-passion, and even more by his trust in telling me the story.

He went on to tell me what happened. It was heartwarming and it was mighty. There had come a remarkable change in the suffering one's prognosis! And that is where a peculiar turn in his testimony occurred. Having told me the circumstance, his prayerful response and what marvelously took place, my friend now seemed to disavow any direct correlation between his action and the results that occurred. Still, though he did not believe Bible-based promises for healing are for today, his family member was now whole. The fact was there with obvious evidence that a wonderful spiritual and physical victory had been won through prayer. Yet, his passion for the Bible's *preciousness* still disallowed his acceptance of the Bible's *present promises*—at least in this regard.

Of course, I rejoiced with him, for he *was* filled with

thanksgiving for God's goodness in sparing the life of a loved one. But I still could not help but feel a tinge of regret. My friend seemed to be unable to accept the simple presence of God's marvels or miracle power today, even though the Word's beauty, fullness and authority compelled his passions in his brilliant teaching mission. His hesitation to simply, candidly acknowledge the marvel of God's healing sadly testifies to a strange "separation of powers" forged by some systems of belief—a wedged separation between God's Word and wonders—His precepts and His power—His promises and His present readiness to fulfill them *all*.

The passion for fullness will not call us to anything less than the same passion for the Scriptures so magnificently and brilliantly manifest in the friend to whom I refer. But I cannot allow myself to settle for just a theory-become-conviction about God's Word only applying to *select* areas of life. God's Word is intended to be authoritative over and incarnated in *all* of life, to the full extent of the revelation of Its truth in the Scriptures and the ministry of our Lord Jesus Christ.

To what degree am I tempted to submit to the fear of accepting God's appeal to me—a biblical call to expect His power-works?

> Call to me, and I will answer and show you great and mighty things, which you do not know . . . Most assuredly, I say to you, he who believes in Me, the works that I do shall he do also; and greater works than these he will do, because I go to My Father (Jeremiah 33:3; John 14:12).

Fervent boldness is called for in the Scriptures as well as foundational belief. We're never told our "call" can force God into action, but neither are we discouraged from *asking* Him *anything*. Still, entrenched systems force an unnatural cleavage between the incredible-though-unpredictable *miracle* power of God and the infallible-and-reliable *promises* of His Word. It's puzzling we are so inclined to fear merging the two: His timeless precepts and His changeless power.

FULLNESS OF THE WORD

Yet, a biblical passion for fullness will be first concerned with the Word of God itself. Signs or wonders may well confirm Its preaching, but the truly passionate will begin with a commitment to knowing the Bible's precepts—*God's will and ways*. Then, having taken that stand, let us appropriate Its power-filled promises—*God's works and wonders*.

As with the Cross—*salvation's fountain*, let us affirm essential basics regarding God's Word—*revelation's fountainhead*. What attitudes ought we verify together, assuring us that our passion for biblical power is as attentive to being *"biblical"* as it is to finding *"power"*? Perhaps these premises will start us on a path of understanding together—keeping our passion for fullness aligned with the wisdom in God's Word.

1. *Let us affirm our trust in the accuracy of the Scriptures.*

The passion for fullness is motivated by a belief in the promises of God's Word, not on the basis of a superficial enthusiasm, but in a settled conviction about the reliability of God's *words* as transmitted to us. The *words* of *the* Word are trustworthy and unmistakenly clear because God Himself has given them to us. Even though human agency has been involved, divine accuracy is undiminished:

> "All scripture is given by inspiration of God, and is profitable for doctrine, for reproof, for correction, for instruction in righteousness" (2 Timothy 3:16).

> "For prophecy never came by the will of man, but holy men of God spoke as they were moved by the Holy Spirit" (2 Peter 1:21).

Even though the passing of these scriptures from generation to generation has involved the complication of human imperfection in copying, Fredriek Kenyon, a leading authority on critical analysis of the literature of the Bible has said:

No fundamental doctrine of Christian faith rests on any disputed reading in any of the manuscripts. Divergences of readings (should not) give rise to the doubt whether the substance, as well as the language of the Bible, is questionable. It cannot be too strongly asserted that the substance of the text of the Bible is certain. Especially is this case with the New Testament. The number of manuscripts of the New Testament, of early translations from it, of quotations from it in the oldest writers of the Church is so large that it is practically certain that the true reading of every doubtful passage is preserved in some one or other of these ancient authorities.

This can be said of no other ancient book in the world. Scholars are satisfied they possess substantially the true text of the principal Greek and Roman writers whose works have come down to us: of Sophocles, of Thucydides, of Cicero, of Virgil, yet our knowledge of their writings depends on a mere handful of manuscripts, whereas the manuscripts of the New Testament are counted by hundreds and even thousands.[1]

We affirm our convictions regarding the *accuracy* of the Scriptures, but still there are some who debate and divide over exactly *how* this conviction ought to be asserted. Preferring to avoid this arena of scholarly debacle, may I suggest we at least receive one another on these terms: *We believe the Bible record about Jesus—His life, His death and His Resurrection?* Let us maximize this assurance while not belittling concerns over which some still debate; affirming our principle conviction, that the Bible's testimony to Christ Himself is perfectly accurate. Here are grounds enough for our beginning.[2]

2. Let us affirm the importance of our study of God's Word.
The call to fullness can never occur in an atmosphere where a shallowness in God's Word is countenanced. Jesus spoke of the Bible as essential to our survival and as crucial to knowing Him:

"Man shall . . . live . . . by every word which proceeds from the mouth of God; . . . Search the scriptures . . . they testify of Me" (Matthew 4:4; John 5:39).

Our posture is to heed the directives the Scripture gives about its use:

- *To read and study it*: "Till I come, give attention to reading, to exhortation, to doctrine" (1 Timothy 4:13); "Be diligent to present yourself approved to God, a worker who does not need to be ashamed, rightly dividing the word of truth" (2 Timothy 2:15).

- *To memorize it*: "Your word I have hidden in my heart, that I might not sin against You" (Psalm 119:11).

- *To honor it*: "More to be desired are they than gold, yea, than much fine gold; sweeter also than honey and the honeycomb. Moreover by them Your servant is warned, and in keeping them there is great reward" (Psalm 19:10, 11).

- *To heed it*: "But be doers of the word, and not hearers only, deceiving yourselves . . . He who looks into the perfect law of liberty and continues in it, and is not a forgetful hearer but a doer of the work, this one will be blessed in what he does" (James 1:22-25).

We need not concern ourselves that different approaches in interpretation exist among believers, or that nuances of doctrine distill from our various approaches to study. Instead, let us revel in our common love for His Word rather than dividing over our use of It. Living truth, revealed in the Scriptures, has one primary purpose: it is not so much given as an instrument of intellectual enlightenment as it is a means of spiritual deliverance. The truth is to *free* us as we study, not to *freeze* us at a distance from one another. To study the Scriptures in a search for Christ within their pages is entirely biblical. However, to dissolve to mere *learning without loving* is to succumb to an antiseptic scholasticism which only accrues information while becoming devoid of the life-giving, life-filling intent of Truth.

3. *Let us affirm our place under the authority of God's Word.*

Subjectivism and relativism have always characterized mankind's quest for truth, and thus, "ever learning they have not been able" to come to its knowledge (2 Timothy 3:7). Once the absolutes of divine revelation are refused, man drifts from truth and wisdom, insisting on his own variable standard—always alterable and dictated by his own whim or convenience.

Such a practice of "defining truth to suit experience" is not to be the practice of the Christian. The Word of God is our absolutely authoritative and solely conclusive standard. And thus, a true passion for fullness, which opens to the experiential dimensions of Holy Spirit power, will *ever* keep God's Word as the authority governing one's discoveries of new anointing and refreshing. For the truly passionate—for *all* fullness—the Bible ever remains the final authority for our faith and our conduct:

> "Continue in the things which you have learned and been assured of, knowing from whom you have learned them, and that from childhood you have known the Holy Scriptures, which are able to make you wise for salvation through faith which is in Christ Jesus. All Scripture is given by inspiration of God, and is profitable for doctrine, for reproof, for correction, for instruction in righteousness" (2 Timothy 3:14-16).

Further, in affirming our submission to the commandments and precepts of the Scriptures, we are wise to equally affirm the conviction that God's Word is *always* intended to be "the perfect law of liberty," and *always* to breathe with "spirit and life" (James 1:25; John 6:63).

The balance of these biblical texts will sustain the authority of the Bible's mandates without giving place to the bondage of human systems of legalism. "For this is the love of God, that we keep His commandments. And His commandments are not burdensome" (1 John 5:3).

THE WORD AND FAITH

In affirming the authenticity and authority of God's Word as being *consistent* with our passion for fullness, let us also affirm our commitment to its active, living power. "For the Word of God is living and powerful, and sharper than any two-edged sword, piercing even to the division of soul and spirit . . ." (Hebrews 4:12).

There is something dynamic about God's Word which has always been renewed and applied in the wake of spiritual awakening. Its *active* power is emphasized in the way the Bible talks about itself.

Any discussion of "passion" and God's Word brings us to face the fact that some earnest souls have stretched the issue of "the Word" and "active faith" to dangerous limits. Segments of the renewal community have given rise to concerns by varied degrees of exaggeration in their seeking a holy dynamism in living. Honesty necessitates admitting that sometimes these emphases have come as a reaction against what has appeared to be a cold, merely analytical use of the Scripture. As clearly as some may seem extreme in forcing their use of God's Word for *power*, others seem to prize the objective truth of the Word to the neglect of appropriating its *power-promises*.

Any evangelical Christian would react to the idea that mere philosophic thoughts about Christ are a sufficient substitute for decisive faith in Him. Similarly, many charismatic believers react toward any passivity they perceive toward the power potential in God's Word and promises. It's true that some zealous souls pirate proof-texts from the Bible's broader presentation of certain truths. The scriptural setting of many promises, which qualify the Word's application, are blindly set aside by many. So being wise to acknowledge these dangers, how may we pursue our passion for all the power in God's Word?

First, as to "faith" and "the Word," let us simply note that, indeed, the Scripture *does* intimately relate them: "So then faith comes by hearing, and hearing by the Word of God" (Romans 10:17).

Further, the Bible links "faith" with both *hearing* and *speaking* the Word of God's promise: "The word is near you, even in your mouth and in your heart (that is, the word of faith which we preach) that if you confess with your mouth the Lord Jesus and believe in your heart that God has raised Him from the dead, you will be saved. For with the heart one believes to righteousness, and with the mouth confession is made to salvation" (Romans 10:8-10).

In short, what the Bible *says* is understandably intended to affect how Its believers *speak*. And yet, from such basic passages, and from out of the fountainhead of God's Word Itself, a passion for the fullness of God's promises has exploded into fiery controversy.

An entire sector of the renewal community has set an agenda which understandably concerns many who perceive a fragmentary use of the Word as crippling to fundamental, healthy, believing life.[3] Sloganized terms have labelled the perceived offenders: "Name it and claim it"; "Health and wealth gospel"; "Faith formula teachers." The terms have been bandied about frequently and stereotypes paraded, all of which urge toward a distancing from such Christians. At the same time, many churches and believers of this stereotyped circle are testifying to a Bible-based, effective and growing life of joy and loving service in Christ as a result of these teachings. Where is a discerning point of distinguishing between the fruitful and the unworthy? Can this be all bad? How can we sort out the difference between a judicious quest for the *power of* the Word without falling into *presumption with* the Word?

First, let us admit that, inescapably present in the texts quoted above, God's Eternal Word does therein give the principles of saving faith:
- Faith is dependent upon God's Word.
- When believed in the heart, the Word is mighty to save.
- When believed in the heart, that belief should be spoken.

It is from these foundational elements that proponents of

"word-faith" teaching have argued that *all* the processes of God's *full* program of salvation are established. In other words, whether the issue is one's salvation or other gifts, graces or promises from the Word, the key for applying God's promises is to "confess"—that is "speak"—them. The idea advances further with the thought that if God's Word is placed upon the lips of His redeemed sons and daughters, It has the same creative power as when He speaks it.

There is something inherent in the underlying truths here that one must be slow to disregard, if not sensitive to study carefully. Still, many evangelicals (including some Pentecostals) have decried the lengths to which this concept has taken a host of Christians. There is certainly some reason for concern. While the label of "cult" has not yet been pinned on the "faith formula" circle of Christians (and certainly shouldn't be) there are signs of needed adjustment. Whatever blessing may have accrued, injuries abound among other adherents:

- Lovelessness and legalism seem to surface too readily, when some treat with condemnation or rejection those who do not "get from God" what they have asked or "claimed."

- The refusal to acknowledge present realities of pain, problem or poverty, as though to observe the obvious with simple honesty will manifest unbelief, smacks of non-Christian mind-science philosophies, or just plain superstition.

- Some approaches in communicating this teaching contribute to a low view of God Himself, seeming to reduce Him to a marionette whose strings must be pulled to get desired action. God is made a "'cosmic bellhop' rather than the 'Sovereign of the Universe.'"[3]

Further, with whatever valid blessing and victory our faith may learn to trust and obey God's Word and discover His financial provision in answer to prayer, it is questionable how well understood biblical promises of prosperity are being balanced.

It would be less than biblical to deny that God does make very practical covenants with His people who will learn the grace of generosity and obedience in giving. And He *keeps* those promises too. But sweeping generalizations about God's "promises of abundance" easily distort the *fullness* of the Word, and the New Testament call to a spirit of sacrifice, self-giving service and communal suffering are often cavalierly overlooked. God's *true* promises of plenty and His will to bless and prosper His people appear at times to be reduced to self-centered slogans and spiritualized get-rich-quick schemes.

The passion for fullness requires that the "faith formula" debate and its problems be addressed. Unresolved, the subject holds the possibility of at least three things occurring—none desirable:

(1) Some well-intended believers will eventually bog down in Bible-distorting confusion in the name of "faith."

(2) Others, rejecting the former, will neglect vital biblical truth and bog down in practical unbelief.

(3) Many of us may withdraw from a passion for God's present works of power; fearing that to pursue them is the equivalent of accepting an approach to "faith" which might result in spiritual presumption and biblical distortion.

Many Christians identify "word-faith" or "faith formula" teaching as the summary definition of what "charismatic" life is all about.

It isn't.

To whatever degree the term "charismatic" may be interpreted by the reader to describe anyone with a passion for God's fullness, it is certainly *not* a call to an imbalanced use of God's Word. Rather, the true passion for fullness includes a passion for a fullness of all God's Word, in the spirit of the three affirmations made earlier (pp. 91-95). Such a "fullness" will help me learn to balance the *objective* truth of the Scriptures with my personal *subjective* appropriation of its promises. I will beware of *either* (1) losing sight of the value of careful study and sound application of the Word, or (2) refusing the spirit of faith inherent in God's Word which calls me to practical faith-in-action.

God *is* seeking people who will lay hold of the *living power* in His Word, who with childlike trust will expect His mightiness. But that is fulfillable without tripping on exaggerations or falling into error. So let us determine to have *all* the fullness of the power inherent in God's Word. Let us refuse to allow *exaggerations* of "faith" to blind us to the fact the Holy Spirit *is* calling the Church to *faith*—vital, active belief in God's living Word of power. Our fullness in the *written* Word needs to be gauged by our fullness of the *living* Word. We need to make room for God to manifest the power of His Word—to let Jesus be Himself, now as at any time. Why *fear* God's promises because some may presume on them? Instead,

- Let us rejoice when people find healing in God's promises. But let our rejoicing be in *Christ*; aware that such instances are not a tribute to *our* faith but to *His* great faithfulness.

- Let us acknowledge God's will and desire to provide for our material needs. But let our giving be in the spirit of *Christ*, who "though He was rich, yet for our sake He became poor, that we through His poverty might be made rich" (2 Corinthians 8:9). The objective of Christlike giving is the wealth of others!

- Let us admit the need for breaking the back of negativism and doubt in the mind and speech of multitudes of Christians. But in speaking God's promises, let our declarations be unto His praise, not a legal performance depending on the power of our consistency in speech. May we, with a heartfelt declaration of praise, sing or speak His promises, but learn in that same spirit to rest in His goodness—whatever comes.

These are timeless and ongoing results of the power of God's

Word when His promises are received and trusting hearts believe them. To believe God's Word and exercise faith in His promise is to *not* give oneself over to self-centeredness, unlovingness, arrogance or reckless use of the Holy Scriptures. Where mishandling of the Word begets those traits we are not witnessing "faith," but the claiming of God's Word as supposed grounds for human systems of presumption.

Let's take the high ground—believing the *whole* of His Word, receiving *all* of His promises and balancing the *entirety* of scriptural truth. It is worth little to expend time attacking those you may perceive as violating biblical balance. Where such exist, they will wither of their own barrenness and lack of root. So instead of becoming carping critics, let us pursue balanced, bold, biblical *believing*! Let's welcome God's *precepts* for our lifestyle and His *promises* for our need.

His *precepts* will beget a holy behavior and manifest Christ's character;

His *promises* will provide a holy sufficiency of gifts and resources for our life and service in His Name.

CHAPTER

9

"Let all the past be but a holy prelude, Lord,
To all the fire and power You now outpour on me.
All Consuming flame, come and overflow me,
And let Thy Kingdom come unto me this hour. J.W.H.

Irresistable Power of Unleashed Holiness

True-hearted passion for fullness puts an absolute priority on personal holiness.

To be filled with the Holy Spirit means to be filled with the One who opens all the possibilities of holiness. The same *regenerating* work which makes us holy before God opens to His *renewing* work to grow us as people of holiness before men. Clear thinking about holiness is essential. It's the key to our avoiding the error anyone may make of pursuing His *power* as an end in itself.

The apostle James seizes an unusual term to stir our attention on this point: "Or do you think that the Scripture says in vain, 'The Spirit who dwells in us yearns jealously?'" (James 4:5).

Jealous.

Think of it! *Jealously*, the Holy Spirit *resents* and is envious of anything that seeks to compete with or crowd out traits of Jesus' personality in ours. Make no mistake—real fullness calls us to real holiness; and the Holy Spirit will not only press toward it, He's

ready to fully enable that real holiness in us. "Holy" is His first
Name!

We also need to see beyond the blindness induced when holiness is *misdefined* and *misapplied*. God's intent in calling us to
holiness isn't to beget a band of purists or prudes, but to unleash
the beautiful dynamic of Christ in each believer's life.

There is an irresistible power inherent in true holiness.

True holiness is not the result of human efforts or enforced
works of holy living. The power of holy living simply flows from a
lifestyle that keeps our human conduits uncluttered by carnality
and untainted by sin. God's love and power simply *happen*, as
rivers of living water flow to fill ordinary believers, and overflow
with pure hope and health to those they meet. "Jesus cried out, 'If
anyone thirsts, let him come to Me and drink. He who believes in
Me, as the Scripture has said, out of his heart will flow rivers of
living water'" (John 7:37-38).

Nothing could be *less* religious or forced than this; nothing could
be *more* beautiful or blessed. Full holiness rises with holy fullness.
"Pure *power*" is Jesus' pure *Person* flowing through the one who
drinks deeply of Himself. Inner channels are dredged of impurity.
Dry places of the soul are flooded with the Spirit from on high.

"This He spoke of the Holy Spirit whom those believing in
Him would receive" (John 7:39). The grace that *saves* not only
cleanses us before God, but awaits within with a reservoir of
potential. Only those thirsty enough for the overflow—for
"*rivers*"—will find the flood gates pushed open by the hand of
God. The passion for more of God, for the power of the Spirit, for
the pure Person of Jesus bursting in, upon and through our lives, is
all that will unleash these streams.

Thirst, not works, determines the recipients of this heavenly
blend of purity and power. The lingering supposition that an
acquired "holiness of life" earns a "balance due" of holy power is a
common but empty idea. God is never indebted to any human
being. All His works are by grace alone. Yet this fact does not
argue against regulatory guidelines of biblical disciplines. While
rejecting any yoke of legalism, we cannot accept a maverick,

unharnessed, self-licensing lifestyle. How often has "grace" been presumed upon by someone *experiencing* God's power-works *by* grace, and yet who persisted in refusing to live *within* grace's expectation of obedience?

Those expectations, while not involving my *works*, do involve my *walk*. If I walk presumptuously, the power-flow generated by the Holy Spirit's grace may continue for a season, but inevitably my life will shipwreck and many "on board" will be devastated by my influence.

In contrast, a beautiful balance may be learned. If I choose to learn to *open* to the Holy Spirit's *power*, and at the same time set myself with a *passion* for *purity*, an awesome unleashing of the power of God's holiness will result. What do we mean by "holiness"?

By definition, God's holiness describes the essential completeness of His being. It is the divine attribute of our Father which keeps Him entirely and totally all that He is. The fullness of His Person, in its beauty, righteousness, love, power and perfection, is due to a completeness which is sustained by His absolute holiness, and thereby guarded from any reduction.

Now the purpose and passion in God's disclosing His holiness toward mankind is not to impress man with His superiority or intimidate him with His supreme sufficiency and perfection. Rather, God's goal is to give His holiness away—as a free gift of completion, to bring His completeness to bear upon our human incompleteness, and to recover us from what we have lost in falling from man's original created state.

Thus God's purpose in pouring His holiness toward man in His Son and by His Spirit, is to *save* us—

- To *restore* all that has been *eaten away* by the locusts of sin;
- To *refill* all that has been *eroded* by the streams of unrighteousness;
- To *rebuild* all that has been *broken down* by the destructiveness of hell's operations; and
- To *recover* all that has been *decayed* by the works of the flesh.

To see this is to begin elevating holiness beyond the mere observation of rules, regulations, and commandments however scriptural they may be. This viewpoint poses no argument against the rightness of expecting every Spirit-empowered believer to live a holy life—ethically, with integrity, and in biblical morality, purity and righteousness. But Jesus demands *more* than that: "Except your righteousness shall exceed the righteousness of the scribes and Pharisees, you will by no means enter the kingdom of heaven" (Matthew 5:20).

In short, purity *alone* is neither a definition nor a guarantee of holiness. The divine objective in pouring forth holiness is *human wholeness*:

- God has poured out His *forgiveness* through the death of His Son, with blood and water gushing from His wounds to *atone* for sin and *restore* to completeness the broken bond intended between Him and man.
- God has poured out His *truth* through His Holy Word to bring *light* to blinded minds and *liberty* to bound souls, with streams of truth to cleanse away the debris of confusion and to sweep in with eternal wisdom upon which a rock-like life can be securely built.
- God has poured out His *Holy Spirit* that those rivers of living water may course through the church like streams through a dam's sluice gates; generating power for vital living, loving service and dynamic ministry—the *whole* church bringing *wholeness* to the whole *world*.

Jesus sets a stark warning before us—calling us to purity but away from Phariseeism. The first begets God's holy works of wholeness, the latter works against that.

CANDIDATES FOR PHARISEEISM?

There has never been a clan of conscientious contenders for holiness like the Pharisees. They were that sect of religious leaders who ruled the Jerusalem scene during Jesus' time. Because they were highly orthodox and meticulously biblical, everything about them cried out "holiness." At the same time, every memory of them screams a warning against their error. While the Pharisees perceived themselves to be God's most reliable proponents— indeed, His *protectors!*—history reveals them to have become His enemies; ultimately conspiring against and condemning His Son while claiming to be serving the heart of His laws. Is it possible I could pursue a passion for God's fullness—of either holiness *or* power—and still become a candidate for Phariseeism? The Pharisees are so sad an evidence of distorting God's intention for holiness. Where did they miss it?

Three traits of Phariseeism are points of vulnerability to the most sincere. Seeing their error in the light of the Word can help us avoid repeating it. They stumbled at three points; in their attitudes about God's *works*, His *Word* and His *will*.

CHAMPIONS OF HISTORY

In Jesus' day there was no one more believing of the great historic works of God than the Pharisees. They were the epitome of excellence in contending for God's glory as the Almighty One of unmatched supernatural power. They stood in firm opposition against the Sadducees, whose liberalism denied the supernatural; ridiculing the promise of a resurrection. The Sadducee's whole unbelieving system symbolizes to this day the materialistic rejection of the supernatural encountered in contemporary religious circles. But in the face of such unbelief about God's power, the Pharisees held holy convictions.

They were champions of history.

Like any of us who hold firm to the historic record of the Scriptures, they believed the supernatural works of God had really happened just as recorded: the Red Sea indeed opened, God indeed spoke from Sinai, Jericho's walls indeed fell, Jonah indeed was swallowed by and then delivered alive from the belly of a giant fish. The Pharisees believed the power-works of God as registered in history and recounted in the Scriptures. However, the problem rose at this point:

*Though they were champions of God's power in history,
they became critics of His power in the present!*

When God's Son entered history and began working God's
supernatural works of power in their midst, their systems of holiness failed. Seeking to protect God from embarrassment, by trying
to control what could be acceptably done and what couldn't, they
imposed their interpretation of the Sabbath on God's works. They
resisted the Spirit of God at work through His Son, disallowing
His right to transcend His own dispensations and work at His
own pleasure. When Jesus exercised supernatural power on the
Sabbath day, the Pharisees attacked Him. Their standards of
holiness mandated the Sabbath observance as a test of holiness.
Their very precise and primly trimmed regulations, which they
thought served God's intent, had lost the capacity for His Sabbath
to mean rest and *wholeness* for mankind. Jesus was rejected for
ministering at the wrong time, or dispensation—on the seventh
day. They preempted a place for a present invasion of His holiness
to manifest in healing the sick or delivering from demons except
on their terms. Though believing God to be supernatural in might,
they confined His works to a calendar which they thought was
theirs to control, and argued for His power to operate either in the
past or the future.

INSISTENT ON INSPIRATION

It is a terrifying thing to see how closely my own beliefs may
align with the underlying convictions of the Pharisees, for they
also completely believed *all* the Bible. The Scriptures of the time—
the Old Testament—were assuredly declared to be the very Word
of God and exact *words* of God. The scribes who transcribed
copies of the Scriptures onto papyri were reverently sensitive.
Handling God's Word was a holy ritual. Every *letter* was deemed
holy—a view which Jesus affirmed Himself, showing His own
equal reverence for the Word when He said, "Not one jot or one
tittle will pass from the law until all is fulfilled" (Matthew 5:18).
"Jot or tittle" referred to the smallest letter and the slightest

punctuation mark, and every part was viewed as important as the whole of the Scriptures—the inspired, holy, eternal Word. And yet, with so commendable a view of the Word of God pre-occupying their studies, we still witness their missing a crucial point in understanding and spirit.

> *Though they were insistent on the inspiration of the Scriptures, they were resistant to the incarnation of the Word.*

Here, with the incarnate Word speaking the life, love and power of God in their midst, their "holiness" blinded their eyes to His nature and purpose. They accused Him of being demonic, charging Him with turning the people from the Law of Moses. Their preoccupation with the *letter* of the Word distracted them from the merciful, healing *life* in Christ, the *living* Word. God's Word had become flesh, and once unleashed from letters which their interpretations could control, they resisted His words *and* deeds, even though all He brought was *wholeness.*

This flaw in the Pharisees' systems unfolds in Matthew's report of Jesus' *ministry* of holiness which stands in dramatic contrast to the Pharisees' *mindset* about holiness.

> And when the men of that place recognized Him, they sent out into all that surrounding region, brought to Him all who were sick, and begged Him that they might only touch the hem of His garment. And as many as touched it were made perfectly well. Then the scribes and Pharisees who were from Jerusalem came to Jesus, saying, "Why do Your disciples transgress the tradition of the elders? For they do not wash their hands when they eat bread." But He answered and said to them, "Why do you also transgress the commandment of God because of your tradition?" (Matthew 14:35-15:3).

The passage pulsates with the tension between insistent literalism and incarnate holiness. For the Pharisees, holiness is clean hands; for Jesus, holiness is whole people. It is a personal warning to me that if I become bent on preserving my tradition, even when supposing I am defending God's Word and values, I may not only miss the intent of the holiness of God, but may fall into the even deeper pitfall of self-righteousness—the ultimate *un*holiness.

Self-righteousness is more than a person's merely trying to save himself by his own works, and far more than the conceited snobbery that is unwilling to acknowledge personal imperfection or failure. Those may be expressions of self-righteousness, but, beyond that, I need to understand that *any* effort of mine is "self-righteousness," when I attempt to do any of God's works in any of my human wisdom or power. Even if those efforts are aimed at pleasing God or protecting His honor, the death knell sounds over the scene where human efforts substitute for God's efficacy. The Pharisees provide a classic case study.

PARTISANS OF PURITY

No one knows her name today, but the Pharisees did. They not only knew her address, they even knew the schedule she kept for her immoral trysts. That's how it was that they arranged to trap her "in the very act" of adultery. They planned to invade her rendezvous of sin to assure their ability to have an actual proven case of adultery to throw at Jesus. The story yields no evidence of any concern for the woman (and where is the man?). The Pharisees' only passion is to press their case against Jesus' kind of holiness.

We all know the story, as the Gospel of John relates it with such penetrating tenderness. The way Jesus handles the situation, as sinfully contrived by the Pharisees as by the two guilty paramours, is a masterful touch displaying His masterly holiness.

The Pharisees intended to demonstrate what they felt was a casual attitude toward holiness on Christ's part. But Jesus answers with such a pure consistency, faithful to both the commandments of God's Word and the heart of God's mercy, His holiness dismantles their case. It shines in its power to deliver and bring a broken sinner to wholeness.

William Barclay calls the account "a story so gracious that for long, men were afraid to tell it,"[1] making this observation while explaining why some early manuscripts do not contain the passage from John, chapter 8. He comments insightfully on the human inclination to seek to "help God" keep people holy, quoting Augustine: "This (episode) was removed from the text of the gospel because some were of slight faith . . . (it was done) to avoid scandal."[2] Why?

Because concern and sincerity over holiness have always demanded a faith in the Holy Spirit to keep people pure. We have all witnessed people who talk "grace," but who take God's gracious love as a license to sin, and make His forgiveness a cheap bauble randomly available for the asking at the whim of the willful and casual sinner. Sensitive souls care about this and readily agree— "We will tolerate no concession to such carnal passivity toward purity."

Still, we are faced with the potential prospect of the Pharisee in us taking over—ready to stone the sinner, assert our superior righteousness and forget God's heart of mercy. Jesus' willingness to be vulnerable to the possibility of violation by any who choose to show indifference toward His holiness, shines from the text. He is perfect in His enforcement of God's justice, yet complete in His offer of God's mercy. He neither condemns nor does He condone. "Neither do I condemn you. Go and sin no more."

In two concise phrases He strikes off the head of any unrepentant will to ongoing sinning and also strikes down any vain hope of the self-righteous at finding a victim to execute. Holiness is both preserved as a value and mediated as a dynamic.

The Pharisees' definition of holiness is confounded—exposed for its *un*wholeness. Their ploy to accuse Jesus' approach to holiness as shallow only reveals their own superficiality. And as they are reduced to helplessness, fleeing from the scene like shamed puppies with their tails between their legs, the Pharisees retreat— still without understanding their foundational problem:

They are partisans of purity,
but they have no heart for true holiness.

This summary of their failure points to the potential of the same twist finding a place in my own system. As a dedicated evangelical believer, I hold to these same three foundational premises as they did:

(a) I believe God is a God of supernatural power;
(b) I believe in the inspiration of the Holy Scriptures; and
(c) I believe in moral purity and holiness of conduct.

The frightening fact is that these Pharisees, holding firmly to these same values, somehow turned these qualifications for holiness into devices of destruction. Staring at their dilemma and my own potential for something of the same misunderstanding, I am driven to the Holy Spirit. As the One who has been given the name and the task for administrating true holiness in me and through me, I need to find a *complete* fullness of His Person—not only His power, but His life-enhancing, warm and wonderful purity.

FULLNESS AND THE HOLY GUEST

Merv Rosell, the beloved evangelist of the generation just passing, used to employ an interesting term for the Holy Spirit. Preaching at a time when the original King James Version of the Bible set the language of the pulpit, and sensing how puzzling it was for some listeners to hear the word "ghost" used for God, he often spoke of the "Holy Ghost" as the "Holy Guest." It was an accurate and effective idea. The Bible not only calls us to welcome His presence reverently as a Guest but assists our understanding of His readiness to be a Helper. Recalling that terminology somehow reminds us of our need to host this Guest, and to seek how we might best respond to *all* His desires.

Just as the passion for fullness focuses on the fullness of salvation and a fullness in God's Word, true holiness in life and service will best grow in a climate where the Holy Guest's ways *and* works are fully welcomed. What are the features of His fullness?

- *He is the Sanctifying Spirit.*

Upon baptizing us into the Body of Christ (1 Corinthians 12:13), and after He has brought new life and a new nature at our new birth (Titus 3:5), the Holy Spirit comes to *grow* us up and *goad* us forward. As Sanctifier, He (1) separates us unto God and His will and (2) commits to work healthy living into us and the unprofitable out of us. Whether you see His work in this capacity as instantaneous or progressive, let us all hold a passion for fullness which affirms our will to have Him fully sanctify us!

- *He is the Fruit-begetting Spirit.*

In our Vine-branch relationship with Jesus Himself, the Holy Spirit is that life-flow emanating to us that brings the character of Christ in us and through us (John 15:1-8). His love is that dominant trait which can produce fruit in increasing ways: "The fruit of the Spirit is love, joy, peace, longsuffering, kindness, goodness, faithfulness, gentleness, self-control" (Galatians 5:22). You've probably memorized the list as I have. But let us not be duped by the notion that in knowing, agreeing with and mentally assimilating it, I am thereby *possessed* of the Holy Spirit. He wants to do that—to possess me; and to fill every corner and abound every fruit. Love is the "life-breath" of all these virtues, and with the Holy Spirit becoming life to our souls as breath is life to our bodies, He will "breathe into" us the excellence of Christ's character in beauty and balance.

- *He is the Revealing Spirit.*

As the Inspirer-Giver of the Word of God, the Holy Spirit is also the Teacher-Applier. Paul prayed for the Ephesians to receive "the spirit of wisdom and revelation" in their knowing and walking with Christ (Ephesians 1:18).

Clearly, he taught that we who have *received* the Holy Spirit need continual and ongoing shaping of our understanding. The

Bible calls such insight into our own need a *"revelation."* These "revelations" are not clever ideas or arcane fancies, but practical spiritual pointers—illuminated insights for our understanding to help us see God's way for us. In this way God-the-Spirit: (1) assures us of His love and (2) advises us of His will. He also keeps *adjusting* us—disallowing our becoming smug or comfortable with the status quo of our souls.

• *He is the Grievable Spirit.*

There is a bittersweet poignancy to this trait of the Holy Spirit's personality. The Bible commands us, "Do not grieve the Holy Spirit by whom you have been sealed unto the day of redemption" (Ephesians 4:30). The verb *lupeo* (grieve) means, "Don't make Him sad; don't cause Him pain." It's a peculiar fact that God, though almighty, has still chosen to render Himself helpless at points before His own creatures. He may be grieved—indeed, in Christ God allowed Himself to be killed! And somehow that fact eloquently warns against a common grief that is caused the Holy Spirit today: *wounding Christ.* Just as Jesus was crucified by unholy hands, the Body of Christ is *still* being speared and spit upon today, and often by its own members. Verbal man-handling and attitudinal lovelessness are ways we may mistreat one another. Of course, this is not the only way I might grieve the Holy Spirit, but one to be sensitive to, because . . .

• *He is the Unifying Spirit.*

"By one Spirit have we all been baptized into one body" (1 Corinthians 12:13). This text declares how in our all having been baptized into Christ, we are called to unity, mutual appreciation and a sensible, gracious interdependency. Yet from this lovely verse, both "one" (unity) and "baptized" have sometimes brought heated debate. "We are 'one'?" asks the Purist. Laboring with fine lines of doctrinal demarcation, he announces: "I can't acknowledge unity with *them.*" Another group isolates the term "baptized with the

Holy Spirit" as applicable only to those meeting their specific experiential criteria. Can the passion for fullness shock us to the truth—and to openness and acceptance of one another in Christ? Certainly it can! Being *filled* with *all* the Holy Spirit's *fullness* can bring His trait as Unifier into our lives at full bloom.

- *He is the Gift-giving Spirit.*

First Corinthians 12 describes the gifts of the Holy Spirit. There are nine—a seeming balance to the nine fruit listed in Galatians 5: word of wisdom, word of knowledge, faith, gifts of healings, working of miracles, prophecy, discerning of spirits, different kinds of tongues, interpretation of tongues.[3] Although His distribution of these gifts to and through Christians is not a second-class manifestation of His grace, how often I have heard it said: "I would far rather have the *fruit* of the Spirit than the *gifts*." Perhaps the spokesman should tell that to the Holy Spirit. I doubt He would concur with our ever-imposing competing priorities where He has *not* proposed or forced a choice. Nothing in the Word of God indicates that either *character* or *charismata*[4] is *pre*ferred or *de*ferred by Him. Rather, the Holy Spirit is calling us all to move in *both* today—His graces and His gifts. The fullness of holiness requires an openness to all His Person, involving all His fruit and all His gifts.

- *He is the Christ-exalting Spirit.*

Jesus prophesied of the Holy Spirit's ministry, "He will glorify Me, for He will take of what is Mine and declare it to you" (John 16:14). There are multiplied ways He does this, but none more consistently or dynamically than by His presence which fills those who open themselves to His work amid the worshiping church. There is a surging reformation in worship sweeping through the global church today. There is nothing more precious than to see the refreshing, renewal, revival *and evangelism* being effected as rising tides of the Holy Spirit have stimulated waves of worship to

Christ in unnumbered thousands of locations. Let's *all* welcome a fullness in worship—allowing the Holy Spirit to stretch us beyond our own self-contained limits.

- Let the informal worshiper invite formal liturgical expressions as well. (A recent extended period of *silence* in our church brought a rich sense of God's presence and power into our midst.)
- Let the more traditional worshiper show a broadened readiness to more spontaneous—and equally scriptural!—exercise of Christ-exalting praise. (Why upraised hands are a fear or a curse to some is biblically unwarranted.)

The Holy Spirit exalts Jesus in many ways—but worship will lead us to them all if we give Him place to expand and enlarge us.

THE WATERSHED POINT

Worship and prayer are the final point to which the passion for "pure power" will bring the sensitive, seeking soul. It will overthrow any disposition in me to restrain or restrict my quest for God by measuring distances between myself and those who respond differently.

Just as worship forms differ and summon us to openness—calling us to be stretched for the inflow of new wine, so will the Holy Spirit confront my temptation to insist on my own private form of receiving His fullness. The watershed point of fullness is at that place where my desire for God precludes my reserving any desire to preserve myself, my system or my style.

Eli judged Hannah negatively for her silence, as she wept before God with a hunger for His grace to beget new life within her (1 Samuel 1:8-18). Some of the throng at Pentecost mocked the 120 disciples as they sounded forth God's praises in tongues they had not learned. One was silent and others were shouting—and both were accused by religious experts of being drunk!

Be careful, soul. The passion for fullness presses me to keep open to God's workings in me. His Word forces me to the wall.

No formulas bring fullness; only passion does. And when the membrane of my soul breaks open, to release the rivers of God's holiness and power, it may manifest itself in Hannah's *tears* or Pentecost's *tongues*—or both. But the floodgates will open and the rivers of the Holy Spirit Jesus promises will gush forth. Don't quench His possibilities by prejudice or restriction. Jesus clearly works in a vast variety of ways. I am wise to be open to them all.

*   *   *   *   *

There is a very telling moment in Jesus' dealings with the disciples—one which underscores this watershed point to which the passion for fullness brings us. It contains a stern warning and points to a simple fact.

The disciples were smugly reporting their having stopped some who were casting demons out "in Your Name," but who were not in their immediate circle. In short, they were saying, "We stopped them because they don't do things our way!" But Jesus immediately corrects them and, setting a child before them, illustrates a point we dare not forget.

Likening those who differ from us to that child, He speaks to our present moment: "And whoever causes one of these little ones who believe in Me to stumble" (i.e., if I wound the soul of a saint I reject), "it would be better for him if a millstone were hung around his neck and he were thrown into the sea" (Mark 9:42).

It's time to let the rivers of prayer, praise and worship rise within by the pure presence of the Holy Spirit. It's time to cease requiring that my experience with God be within some prescribed limits which will assure I do not respond like those of another circle—ones who minister in Jesus' Name, but are not of my chosen fellowship. Jesus' use of the child in teaching His lesson shows that maturity is not my qualification for fullness—simplicity is.

So, let us come and pour out our hearts in worship and prayer.

Let us be open to His purity and power and be done with all the smallness of soul. The excessive baggage of pride and prejudice only drags my soul down—away from the streams of Holy Spirit purity and power.

A millstone is a very uncomfortable necklace.

It's the cumbersome jewelry of any fearful reserve or Pharisaical pretension. It may appear to decorate my flesh, but the ornaments of my own demands only drown my soul in a sea of self-centeredness.

Compared to the "rivers" of the Holy Spirit's flowings, those sea "depths" are shallows.

I not only want to be free of millstones, I want to steer clear of all sandbars of secret reserve.

The surging streams of Holy Spirit-born prayer will flush out flesh and open the channels of His power, unleashing the irresistible power of His holy fullness.

By His grace and for His glory.

Hallelujah!

CHAPTER

10

Above and beyond all the bounds of time and space;
Above early limits, beyond this world's embrace.
A life may be found which with pow'r will abound,
  If you believe
  You can receive
    Power to live, above and beyond.

Christ Jesus the Lord wants to fill your life with love.
The blest Holy Spirit He'll shower from above.
His pow'r He'll impart if you'll open your heart,
  Receive now His gift
  And He will lift
    Your life above and beyond.   J.W.H.

The Passion in Prayer ... Above and Beyond

I had made up my mind. When I got to my dorm room I was going to do it. Even though the picture of myself kneeling beside my bed with my face in a pillow looked funny in my mind's eye, I decided I wasn't going to be intimidated by my own imagination. Regardless how silly it might seem to anyone else, I wasn't going to be threatened by the sound of my own voice again.

What I was facing was a problem in praising.

Most of my church background had been in sound, Bible-centered Christianity, and I had little lack for *knowing* the truth. But suddenly I had come into a setting where an additional factor forced a decision. I was now at a college where the atmosphere not only pressed my Christian commitment to the Word of God with serious academic requirements, but a climate of open, forthright praise and worship prevailed.

At first I had justified my own reserve by mentally arguing that my disposition was different than most of the other students—that they "needed" that kind of expression, but I didn't. But after two weeks of being surrounded by the situation, with no one issuing requirements or treating me any differently, I had come to a point of honesty with myself. My reserve was not a personality trait, it was a private domain I was beginning to fiercely protect. No one was wrestling me on the point, except . . . could it be the Holy Spirit?

Little by little I began to see that the problem was twofold. First, *fear:* I was afraid of becoming something other than what I perceived myself as wanting to be. Second, *uncertainly:* I didn't know how to break the syndrome of my own reserve, feeling that the expressive-yet-orderly praise which surrounded and summoned me was somehow beyond my abilities.

At the bottom line, I was coming to terms with *passion*—the will to extend and expend; to be stretched and to be spent.

That's when I made up my mind.

Quite frankly, it was incredibly simple, although it required a solid decision and a mindset to confront myself. Alone. In my room. And it was there, after a few moments of a prayerful preamble, when I humbly told my Lord Jesus that I wanted to be freed from the foolishness of my own fears of forthright praising, that I buried my head in my pillow so as not to disturb the whole dorm, and I shouted as loudly as I could.

"Hallelujah!

"Praise the Lord!

"Glory to the Name of Jesus!"

After several other exclamations, I began to laugh. With a freeing sense of relief and release, I literally laughed out my next remarks to the Savior: "Lord Jesus, thank You for understanding me and being so patient with my fears. Thank You for setting me free from my *self*—my self-preserving concern over how I appear to others."

My release was in that joy. But my relief was in the glad discovery of what I should have known all along—that to "let go" in openhearted praise isn't to lose control, but simply to surrender that control to Christ. And that praise was the entry point for my release unto impassioned prayer, for from that point, bolder praise and worship opened to fuller dimensions. It didn't reduce or remove my appreciation for the practice of the more reserved and equally valid worship practices I had already known; it only broadened my horizons without narrowing my mind.

For one moment I risked doing something embarrassing, but only to myself . . . and only in private. The reward was immediate, but the fruit has been lifelong in growing upward and going forward. It was a breakthrough in passion, and from there the application became more practical in my prayer-life than anywhere else. Praise is but a doorway: "Enter His gates with thanksgiving and His courts with praise" (Psalm 100:4). But prayer is a *pathway*, and as that passion in praise broke through the wall of my fears, it brought a practical *new* passion—a passion *for* prayer and in prayer.

It is *unto* prayer and *into* prayer that the passion for fullness ultimately leads and only can be satisfied.

Spiritual breakthrough and personal expansion must exceed the "idea" stage—the realm of being only a general "possibility." When *truly* gripped by the passion for fullness, it will lead to its pursuit in prayer. A full exposure of myself to Jesus Himself is the only way to acknowledge my thirst, stretch the wineskin of my own soul and allow a flexible readiness within to receive new wine.

Jesus described the connoisseur's judgment on new wine, always to say, "The old is better." He didn't even deny it. What has been refined, mellowed and aged *is* better. In personal experience we agree; when our hearts have been blessed, when we've received, retained and assimilated a truth, a practice, or a biblical point of maturity, we like it—*it's good!* And because we like what we like, we would prefer it unchanged.

But Jesus' "new wine" message challenges this propensity toward any crustiness and inflexibility invading our souls. Wine is only the analogy—the Holy Spirit is the issue, and thus He presses against settling for sameness. He won't let me secure myself in the familiar, the tame or the comfortable, which might restrict my availability to the Holy Spirit's new creative workings.

There is new wine for *every season* in God's global operations.

- Not new truth, but an untasted flavor within the cluster.
- Not new light, but a heretofore unperceived flash of color on the spectrum.

When Jesus asks, "Will you openly sample something of the 'new wine' I can pour in you?" I suggest we be willing to respond affirmatively: "Amen, Lord. I'll drink to *anything* that *You* want to do!"

So, concluding our call to a passion for fullness, let us come to passionate prayer.

Fullness in God's Spirit—purity and power in life and ministry—are not the products of reasoned discourse or learned research. Words and thoughts can only *confront* our need, *correct* our thinking, and *confirm* our hopes as biblically based. But ultimately I must press beyond precept to a pursuit of God's power in my life.

This is no mere quest for something giddy but of something godly. Our seeking is not a search for a sensual "quick fix," as though being filled with God were nothing more than an injection of a divine drug. Rather, our pursuit of power is a quest to plunge deeper into God Himself!

Reinhard Bonnke, the German evangelist whose crusades under the miracle touch of the Holy Spirit are rocking cities throughout Africa, penetrating parliaments and impacting the leadership of nations with the force and fire of fullness of Jesus Christ's message and power, recently wrote: "God is not only measuring the length of the furrow you plow, but the depth." Those words call us to be stretched and deepened; *unto a fullness of the Spirit that brings a fullness of Jesus' character, that blossoms in His love and purity in our character and bears the fruit of His power and works in our service!*

1. Let prayer stretch and deepen our passion for *Fruitfulness.*

Addressing a group of church leaders, Robert Murray McCheyne spoke to their profession words which can equally speak to anyone in any enterprise. Translate his words regarding "preaching" or "sermons" to your vocation or place in life. Note my parentheses, and insert your personalized point of understanding, pointing up how desperately true it is, that *prayer is the key to fruitfulness.*

"Study universal holiness of life. Your whole usefulness depends on this, for your (sermons) last but an hour or two; your life (preaches) all the week. If Satan can only make a covetous (minister) a lover of praise, of pleasure, of good eating, he has ruined your (ministry).

"Give yourself to prayer, and get your (texts), your thoughts, your words from God. Luther spent his best three hours in prayer."[1]

2. Let prayer stretch and deepen our passion for *Souls.*

The fullness of holiness is to make us instruments of wholeness to reach into a broken world. In a generation where we master the computer, how few have heard of how one man penetrated the Pennsylvania wilderness in the 1700s? Before the development of that colony, David Brainerd shook the native Indian population by the power of the Holy Spirit in prayer. Animistic, paganized peoples, exposed to alcohol by traders from Europe, were won with nothing more or less than a passion for the lost pouring forth in prayer. Only then did Brainerd's preaching find effective entry into the blinded hearts of many as his words, relayed through an unconverted Indian interpreter, garnered a harvest in an impossible setting.

"Let us often look at Brainerd in the woods of America pouring out his very soul before God for the perishing heathen without whose salvation nothing could make him happy. Prayer—secret, fervent, believing prayer—lies at the root of all personal godliness . . . .

A mild (controlled) and winning temper, a heart given up to God in closet religion—these are the attainments which, more than all knowledge, or all other gifts, will fit us to become the instruments of God in the great work of human redemption."[2]

3. Let prayer stretch and deepen our passion for *Purity*.

As we move into Millennium III, A.D., the beckoning of the Holy Spirit is a call to *all* of Christ. But just as we would have no salvation from sin without a sinless Savior, there will be no driving back of the blackness of darkness over the world without a holy church. Jesus' power and wonder works were mighty then and are available by His unchanging mightiness today. But the lasting impact, which will ensue upon our penetration of the world with lightning shafts of miracle power, will be the solid footings laid in a holiness which rightly represents Christ's Person as it mightily reveals His power.

"Be sure you look to your secret duty; keep that up whatever you do. The soul cannot prosper in the neglect of it. Apostasy generally begins at the closet door. Be much in secret fellowship with God. It is secret trading that enriches the Christian.

"Pray alone. Let prayer be the key of the morning and the bolt at night. The best way to fight against sin is to fight it on our knees."—Philip Henry[3]

4. Let prayer stretch and deepen our passion for *Power*.

May all doubt, fear and doctrinaire posturings on *any* side come to a conclusion on this matter. Jesus is mighty—to save, to heal, to expel demons, to work miracles, to manifest signs and wonders. He is waiting to display His holy might at dimensions unprecedented in church history—both in the scope and in the manner of His works. "Look among the nations and watch—be utterly astounded! For I will work a work in your days which you would not believe though it were told you" (Habakkuk 1:5).

We are not venturing on thin ice nor sowing ideas in shallow soil in welcoming *all* the Holy Spirit's works to confirm *all* God's Word as we declare *all* Christ's love to *all* this world. The hour has come to unleash the irresistible power of the Holy Spirit, without fearful reserve and with faith-filled expectancy. A century ago, Charles H. Spurgeon prayed for it. He said:

> The fullness of Jesus is not changed, then why are our works so feebly done? Pentecost—is that to be a tradition? The reforming days—are these to be memories only? I see no reason why we should not have a greater Pentecost than Peter saw, and a Reformation deeper in its foundations, and truer in its upbuilding than all the reforms which Luther or Calvin achieved. We have the same Christ, remember that. The times are altered, but Jesus is the Eternal, and time touches Him not . . . .

With this summons a growing body of historic and recent scholarship beckons us all to a fearless welcoming of God's works of power attending God's Word.

In 1750, John Wesley made this entry in his journal:

> Wed. 15—By reflecting on an odd book which I had read in this journey, 'The General Delusion of Christians with regard to Prophecy,' I was fully convinced of what I had long suspected, 1. That the Montanists, in the second and third centuries were real, scriptural Christians; and, 2. That the grand reason why the miraculous gifts were so soon withdrawn, was not only that faith and holiness were well nigh lost; but that dry, formal, orthodox men began even then to ridicule whatever gifts they had not themselves, and to decry them all as either madness or imposture.[4]

More recently, in his commentary on John's Gospel, Leon Morris expounds Jesus' words concerning His own miracles ministry. Though assailed by Pharisaical ridicule, Christ unabashedly appeals to the testimony of the Scriptures (precepts in the Word) *and* the confirmation of His miracles (power works by the Spirit).[5] Morris footnotes the passage, quoting Bishop Ryle: "We should observe (re: John 10:25) how our Lord always and confidently appeals to the evidence of His miracles. Those who try to depreciate and sneer at miracles, seem to forget how often they are brought forward as good witnesses in the Bible. *This, in fact, is their great object and purpose.*" (Emphasis mine.)[6] Dr. Morris adds, "The general attitude toward miracles in modern times should not blind us to the significance such 'works' held for the New Testament writers."[7]

In succession, Wesley (eighteenth century), Ryle (nineteenth century), Morris (twentieth century), remark on the propriety of our concern that unbelief *not* shear the miraculous from the church's arsenal of resources for spiritual warfare. Now in the 21st century, we are being reminded again; fear and resistance are melting and, with truth setting us free, the Spirit is stirring us to receive His fullest working for this hour of such significance and need.

A DEMANDING DECISION

Here is our summons: may we rise to answer it! Let us decide now—*to commit ourselves to a supernatural ministry, disciplined by a crucified life.*

We need both—power from God and brokenness before Him. Man cannot contain the glory of God in his frail earthen vessel unless he lives in the shadow of the Cross. Is it possible that we can experience a balanced ministry that combines Holy Spirit power and Christ-like character? It is, if we will accept the terms of this demanding decision.

It is demanding because some may relish deeper teaching at the expense of a surging movement of the Holy Spirit, while some may prefer the intoxicating atmosphere of the Spirit's power working at the expense of a genuine humility and holiness of heart.

But the choice need not be between one and the other. A passion for a ministry including the miraculous may be equally passionate in its discipline toward holiness of character and a steadfast, sensible application of systematic truth taught from the Word of God.

The New Testament reveals that this balance is possible: "And with great power the apostles gave witness to the resurrection of the Lord Jesus. And great grace was upon them all" (Acts 4:33).

Notice it: "great power . . . great grace": power-filled, but under the control of in-wrought graces tempering the life with a gentleness of spirit.

Will your heart join mine in passionate prayer? "God, give us a sane, solid and a sensible revival of New Testament power. *Sane,* but not restricted by man's intellectual limits; *solid,* but not unmovable by the breath of the Spirit; *sensible,* but not to the quenching of the Spirit's genuine, valid operations."

There's a call out today for a new band of people who will move "above and beyond," to demonstrate both the dynamic and the compassion—the power and the purity—of Jesus Christ our Lord. That call may seem beyond me, but as I listen, I know the ancient word holds true today: "'Not by might, nor by power, but by My Spirit,' says the Lord of hosts" (Zechariah 4:6). To commit to call out for "all the fullness of God" will be to draw on God's guarantee to answer that cry.

*　　*　　*　　*　　*

In his outstanding little book *Warring Faith*, L. Carter illustrates the reward of unquestioning obedience by relating an incident from the legend of the last days of King Arthur. Arthur was dying, and Sir Bedivere was the only knight remaining with him.

"Take my sword Excalibur," said he. "Throw it as far as you can fling it towards the center of the lake."

The moon was shining brightly above, and in the moonlight the jewels in the handle of Excalibur looked very rich and beautiful, so rich and so beautiful that Sir Bedivere was dazzled by their beauty and he felt he could not throw the sword into the water. He hid it among the reeds, and went, empty-handed, back to the king.

"Did you throw the sword into the lake?" asked King Arthur eagerly.

"Yes, sire," answered Sir Bedivere boldly.

"What happened?"

"Nothing happened, sire!"

The king lay back again with a groan. "Faithless messenger!" he said. "You have not thrown the sword! Go! Do as I command."

Again Sir Bedivere went, but again the beauty of Excalibur overcame him. He returned to the king and declared that he had flung the sword into the water, but still nothing had happened.

Arthur looked at him steadily, and his eyes made Sir Bedivere afraid. "You are not speaking the truth!" cried the king. "Go! Do as I command."

Stung by the king's words, Bedivere rushed down to the lake, and without any hesitation, not daring to look at its beauty, he flung the sword far, far into the lake. Immediately an arm was raised out of the water and grasped the sword. Three times the hand waved Excalibur in the moonlight—then both arm and sword disappeared, and all was still. Breathless and awed, Sir Bedivere went back to the king, and told him what he had seen.

"It is well!" said Arthur. "It is well!"[8]

Christian friend . . . fellow servant: the times press into focus the command of our King, to enter today's spiritual conflict in the full resources of the Holy Spirit. To respond may well mean to become willing to hurl ourselves upon the altar of God—to open to new territory being gained within our hearts that new victories be won throughout the world. Have you ever gone forth as I have, to do His will, and then upon returning heard the whisper of the Master in your soul, "Did you go as I told you?"

"Yes, Lord, I think so."

But then as Arthur inquired of Bedivere, He asks, "What happened?" And knowing that nothing supernatural did happen, my heart feels again the inadequacy of my powerlessness and my need for more of God. But now He's sending us again, and the opportunity for obedience is freshly available. If we will abandon ourselves to Him—cast ourselves before Him at His command—I believe we may share in reality the experience of Bedivere in the myth.

- *Deciding* to overcome our enchantment with ourselves—with that which we so prize of appearance, style or carnal security;
- *Abandoning* ourselves to the above and beyond—hurling ourselves over the waters of human need;

may cost something of what we have too much treasured. But this one thing is sure: if we will cast ourselves forth in obedience, without concern for the cost, the result will always be the same.

We will see a manifestation of the arm of the Lord.

He will display all Christ's fullness to enable our ministry to all man's brokenness, and the passion for fullness shall be fully satisfied . . .

. . . In Christ's heart—as His church ministers in His likeness and power,

. . . And in ours—as His glory fills our lives.

ENDNOTES

Chapter 1
1. E.M. Bounds, *Power Through Prayer*, (originally titled, *The Preacher and Prayer*), The Christian Library, Westwood, New Jersey, 1984.

Chapter 2
1. *The Saturday Evening Post*, 1963.
2. Lausanne Committee for World Evangelism, *Lausanne Covenant*, Article 14, Lausanne Committee for World Evangelism, Wheaton, Illinois, 1974.
3. Martyn Lloyd-Jones, *Joy Unspeakable*, Harold Shaw Publishers, Wheaton, Illinois, 1985, pp. 265, 278.
4. David B. Barrett, ed., *World Christian Encyclopedia*, Oxford University Press, Oxford, 1982.
5. David B. Barrett, "The Twentieth-Century Pentecostal Charismatic Renewal in the Holy Spirit, With Its Goal of World Evangelism," in *Dictionary of Pentecostal and Charismatic Movements*, eds. Stanley M. Burgess and Gary

B. McGee, Zondervan Publishing House, Grand Rapids, Michigan, 1988, p. 811.
6. Barrett, pp. 812-813.
7. C. Peter Wagner, *Regency Reference Library*, Zondervan Publishing House, Grand Rapids, Michigan.
8. Gerhard Friedrich, ed. *Theological Dictionary of the New Testament*, vol. VI, translated and edited by Geoffrey W. Bromiley, William B. Eerdmans Publishing Co., Grand Rapids, Michigan, 1968, pp. 298-305.

Chapter 3
1. V. Raymond Edman, *They Found the Secret*, Zondervan Publishing House, Grand Rapids, Michigan, 1984.
2. Ibid.

Chapter 5
1. I submitted this chapter to Dr. Harold Fickett for his approval, correction or rejection. He wrote in return, "My reaction?—I say 'Amen' both to the accuracy of the illustration and to the interesting way in which you shared it. Your conclusion also hit the nail right on the head. Wouldn't it be wonderful if every believer not only accepted these conclusions but also was motivated by them? Tragically, such is not the case. Perhaps this is the reason the late Mahatma Ghandi once said that he would be a Christian if he could see one."
2. C.S. Lewis, *The Silver Chair*.

Chapter 8
1. Josh McDowell, *Evidence That Demands a Verdict*, Campus Crusade for Christ, Inc., 1972, pp. 45-46.
2. The author does not mean to appear casual toward critical issues that involve attitudes toward the inspiration of the Scriptures. He is personally committed to a belief in the plenary verbal inspiration of the Bible as revealed in the autographs of the Scriptures. Nonetheless, he pleads here

for a broader acceptance of one another, persuaded that in that spirit a thorough scholarly solution is more apt to be found than in a hostile climate which overlooks our grounds for loving one another in Christ.
3. William Menzies' review of D. R. McConnell's book, *A Different Gospel*, *Christianity Today*. March 3, 1989.

Chapter 9
1. William Barclay, *The Daily Study Bible*, Gospel of John, vol. 2, The Westminster Press, Philadelphia, Pennsylvania, p. 336.
2. Barclay, p. 336.
3. While there are dozens of "spiritual gifts" in the Scriptures given by the Godhead, there are only these nine directly mentioned as being "distributed" by the Holy Spirit at His discretion.
4. *Charismata* is the Greek word for gifts; its root *charis* (grace) focuses on the unearned "gift" nature of these operations.

Chapter 10
1. E.M. Bounds, *Power Through Prayer*, The Christian Library, Westwood, New Jersey, p. 7.
2. E.M. Bounds, p. 21.
3. E.M. Bounds, *Purpose in Prayer*, The Christian Library, Westwood, New Jersey, p. 9.
4. John Wesley, *Wesley's Journal*, p. 204, Wed., Aug. 15, 1750.
5. John 5:39, 46; 5:36; 10:25.
6. Leon Morris, *The New International Commentary on the New Testament, Gospel of John*, William Eerdmans Publishing Company, Grand Rapids, Michigan, p. 520.
7. Leon Morris, p. 520.
8. L. Carter, *Warring Faith*.

ACKNOWLEDGMENTS

Some books have pictures which illustrate the story or give visual dimension to the facts therein. Many more include a picture of the author and some brief record of his or her background. But virtually every book, if mention is made at all, gives but a few words in acknowledging those who were pivotal in its being brought into existence. That's understandable, because most who read not only do not know those whose devotion, talent and labor has been expended, but have more interest in reading the book than about how it was produced. Still, I wish there were a way, in acknowledging and thanking the following people, to let you see them, know them as people, and appreciate at least a small amount of why I feel so great an indebtedness to them.

Deepest thanks to —

... those at Word who believed in, nourished and brought the project to completion: Kip Jordon, Al Bryant and especially Ernie Owen;

... those at my office who so constantly attend to details which make my writing ministry possible: Janet Kemp, Sandy Turner, Lana Duim and especially Renee McCarter and Susanne Mahdi, whose typing and editorial assistance were crucial on this book;

... the Pastoral Team and Deacon-Elder body of our congregation, who steward the Word and shepherd the flock beside me, and whose strong servant-leadership allows me time to serve in ways I hope this book might; and

... as always, to Anna, who with patience and understanding prayed me through this "most-demanding-so-far" book of mine. As it has been completed we have both experienced a role-reversal of sorts; since I now think I might understand the travail of childbirth a little better—and since now she knows she understands the prayer-filled and frustrating sense of helplessness in standing beside a struggling form seeking to bring forth new life.

I hope the book might contribute to that—to new life. And if it does, I apologize for your not having a set of pictures of those who made it possible.

Jack W. Hayford